The

WEED
AGENCY

ALSO BY JIM GERAGHTY

Voting to Kill

The

WEED AGENCY

A COMIC TALE OF FEDERAL BUREAUCRACY WITHOUT LIMITS

JIM GERAGHTY

CROWN
FORUM
NEW YORK

Published in the United States by Crown Forum, an imprint of the Crown Publishing Group, a division of Random House LLC, a Penguin Random House Company, New York.
www.crownpublishing.com

CROWN FORUM with colophon is a registered trademark of Random House LLC.

Library of Congress Cataloging-in-Publication Data
Geraghty, Jim.
  The weed agency : a comic tale of federal bureaucracy without limits /
Jim Geraghty.
       pages cm
  1. Political fiction. 2. Satire. I. Title.
  PS3607 E726W44 2014
  813'.6—dc23

                                                    2013048933

ISBN 978-0-7704-3652-0
eBook ISBN 978-0-7704-3653-7

Cover design by Michael Nagin
Cover illustration by Owen Richardson

First Edition

146028962

To Allison,

for more than anyone will ever know

AUTHOR'S NOTE

A careful review of the Federal Register for the past thirty years will reveal that the U.S. Department of Agriculture Agency of Invasive Species does not, *technically*, exist.

However, the Federal Interagency Committee for the Management of Noxious and Exotic Weeds, the Aquatic Nuisance Species Task Force, and the Federal Interagency Committee on Invasive Terrestrial Animals and Pathogens are very real. And the USDA does play a key role in the federal National Invasive Species Council, along with the Environmental Protection Agency, U.S. Agency for International Development, NASA, the Department of Homeland Security, and eight other federal departments and agencies.

In short, each time in the following pages you encounter an anecdote that seems too wildly implausible to actually be a funded and officially authorized activity of the federal government, rest assured that the tale you are reading does not overstate such things; if anything, the sheer scope of such inexplicable and odd expenditures is understated for the sake of storytelling.

The gargantuan, ever-growing, ever-less-accountable, impossible-to-uproot federal bureaucracy is actually the sleeper issue of our time. It's at the heart of the conservative critique of modern government: faceless bureaucrats writing incomprehensible regulations that complicate our lives for no good reason.

But if you put enough drinks—or sodium pentothal—in

a liberal, they'll usually admit that they find the federal government's performance to be deeply disappointing. They envision so many ways that government can improve the lives of citizens, and enact program after program pursuing those goals . . . only to find money wasted, deadlines missed, departments and agencies burning through their budgets, complicated forms, and a mess of structures and procedures that even Rube Goldberg would feel an urge to simplify.

In my lifetime, three waves of Republicans came to Washington pledging to cut red tape and eliminate waste—the Reagan wave, the Gingrich wave, and the Bush wave—and all of them largely failed. Bill Clinton and Barack Obama arrived, full of ideas of how government could "put people first" and "work smarter" . . . with little to show for it. In some ways, the fight of the Left vs. the Right is the undercard fight. The real showdown—certain to intensify in the budget fights to come—is the Permanent Bureaucracy vs. Everyone Else.

The monetary waste is scandalous enough, but there's a human waste, too. Despite the current zeal for demonizing Washington, each year thousands of young people come to the nation's capital, eager to make the world a better place. Many of them end up working for the federal government—and utilizing only a fraction of their potential, often hammered into accepting a role as a cog in a large, self-propelled, unstoppable machine dedicated to its own perpetuation. The Man in the Gray Flannel Suit works in the public sector now.

In September of 2004, a headline in the *New York Times* proclaimed:

Memos on Bush Are Fake but Accurate, Typist Says

So if, indeed, "fake but accurate" is a classification good enough for the esteemed pages of the *New York Times*, then what you are about to encounter in this story—characters whose existence has not been proven, witnessing historical events and interacting with actual lawmakers and high-level officials who have populated our nation's capital since the early 1980s—can accurately portray the truth of how the government works . . .

—Jim Geraghty

1

FEBRUARY 1981

U.S. National Debt: $950 billion

Budget, USDA Agency of Invasive Species: $20.2 million

J ack Wilkins knew he was about to witness history: In the long history of budgetary fights, Adam Humphrey vs. Nicholas Bader was going to be the clash of the titans: Otto von Bismarck vs. Genghis Khan.

At stake was nothing less than the existence of the federal agency that employed Wilkins and Humphrey, the U.S. Department of Agriculture's Agency of Invasive Species. President Jimmy Carter established the agency, dedicated to protecting American agriculture and gardens from the menace of invasive weeds, just four years earlier, and it stood out as a most likely target for cuts.

Humphrey's official title at the agency was abbreviated as "USDA DFS BARM A-IS AD,"[1] but as the administrative director, the highest-ranking non-appointed position, agency employees considered him the only man within the agency who actually knew what was going on.

---

1 U.S. Department of Agriculture, Department of Farm Services, Bureau of Agricultural Risk Management, Agency of Invasive Species, Administrative Director.

And yet, as the two men sat in Humphrey's office in the U.S. Department of Agriculture building in Washington, Wilkins found his boss oddly quiet and almost too confident.

"We have a week to save our jobs," Wilkins emphasized. He wasn't surprised that his boss didn't share his panic—Humphrey was legendarily unflappable—but unnerved that his boss seemed so engrossed by the articles about the incoming Reagan administration's budget hawks that he seemed oblivious to the notion that their own jobs were among those they would try to cut.

"I thought that Gergen, Stockman, and the other barbarians coming in with the president would give us more time, but they just called and asked us to meet with Nick Bader Monday morning." Wilkins exhaled. "Of all the folks we could deal with, Bader's the worst. 'Nick the Knife.' 'Big, Bad Bader.'"

Like most of Washington, Wilkins thought that "President Ronald Reagan" was a fanciful, silly notion that the electorate would never actually indulge as an experiment. But the 1980 election hadn't even been that close, and now the early days of the administration revealed an even more unthinkable development: Reagan and his team hadn't merely been *talking* about cutting the government; they were putting together a budget that would actually do it. The twenty-six-year-old Wilkins had jumped to the high-ranking assistant administrator position at the federal agency after reaching early burnout in the Carter White House, and now what he had been assured was a remarkably safe civil service job felt precarious.

Humphrey was only a decade older than Wilkins but the difference felt generational. Unlike Wilkins's deepening anxiety, Humphrey shrugged off the incoming administration's pledge to cut wherever possible; he had recently tried to reassure his younger assistant that those who pledge to uproot bureaucracy are among those most likely to succumb to it. He pointed out that the president arrived in Washington with forty-eight separate task forces assigned to assist in the effort to reorganize the government, with more than 450 eager minds, mouths, and egos involved. The overall government-cutting bible of the merry band, *Mandate for Leadership*, published by the Heritage Foundation, was a 1,093-page book that represented the work of twenty task forces with three hundred participants, some of whom overlapped with Reagan's task forces.[2] The president's inner circle selected the dangerous right-winger David Gergen to set up the president's Initial Actions Project with a forty-nine-page report laying out the plan to not get distracted in his first year in office.

Despite Humphrey's quiet, inexplicable confidence, the Reagan team moved quickly and his little kingdom—a federal agency assigned the silly-sounding duty of ensuring the nation's safety from invasive weeds—stood out, glaringly, high on the list of potential cuts.

The decisive meeting with the administration loomed a week away, with every expectation that the session would end with the administration announcing its intent to eliminate the Agency of Invasive Species entirely.

Wilkins had hoped the meetings would be with someone reasonable, someone like David Stockman, the congressman who was leaving the Hill to become Reagan's new head of the White House Office of Management and Budget. Instead . . .

Bader.

No name struck more fear into the hearts of government employees than the newly named Special Assistant to the President for Budgetary Discipline Nicholas Bader. Among federal employees, Bader was deemed slightly more threatening and evil than Charles Manson. Bader was jealous of Stockman's

---

2   Steven Hayward, *The Age of Reagan*, p. 47.

reputation as the administration's most fearsome axman, and shortly after a *Newsweek* cover piece on Stockman, Bader cooperated with a *Time* profile on himself that called him, "Reagan's bloody right hand, always grasping a meat cleaver and craving the chance to cut deeper and faster." The accompanying caricature portrayed him as Jack the Ripper.

In a heavy-handed symbolism rarely found outside Herblock cartoons, slain women labeled with various government agencies' three-letter acronyms were depicted lying at Bader's feet as his head was thrown back, roaring with laughter. The comparison didn't bother Bader in the slightest; he joked that the cartoonist intended the comparison of government agencies to prostitutes.

A *Time*'s reporter asked Bader what, if any, government spending was legitimate and necessary. The pugnacious Reaganite instantly and easily replied that at this moment in American history, all government resources should be refocused upon the threat of the Soviet Union, now on the march in Afghanistan and who knows where next.

· · ·

One week later, Wilkins felt even less assured about the upcoming budget battle, and Humphrey's mysterious confidence continued unabated. They met at the agency offices in the Department of Agriculture building at 14th Street and Independence Avenue, then grabbed a cab for the short ride to Bader's lair in the Old Executive Office Building. Humphrey never walked in winter.

On the cab's radio, Pat Benatar dared her suitors to demonstrate their marksmanship.

"So the plan is, what, Adam, hypnotize him?" asked Wilkins, fidgeting with the handle on his briefcase.

"Relax, Jack," Humphrey instructed. "Bader feeds off of anxiety, and if you show weakness, suggest any concession, he will pounce. He will begin with bluster and an attempt to demonstrate dominance to set the tone of the meeting, like a great ape beating his chest. Ignore it all and appear unimpressed. Let me do the talking. And concur with anything I say."

Wilkins nodded, and nervously cracked his knuckles.

. . .

Bader himself drove in from the Virginia suburbs. Despite his reputation as part of the Reaganite preppie vanguard, he had a soft spot for pop music. British rockers singing about one after another biting the dust put him in the appropriately ruthless mood for the workday.

He drummed the steering wheel and wiggled his tush to the beat in the driver's seat, amusing the occasional commuter in the next lane. Next to the perpetually sunny president, Bader enjoyed his job more than anyone else in Washington.

The grandson of German immigrants, Bader grew up in Queens, New York, in a thoroughly middle-class lifestyle, the son of an accountant father and aspiring entrepreneurial mother.

Young Nick had learned to give his father, Reynard P. Bader, CPA, a wide berth from about mid-January to mid-April. Life returned to its relaxed and warm tone after the last of those who had filed extensions had submitted their paperwork. Mastering the ever-more-complicated tax code, coupled with the unpleasant news of telling other people how much they owed, tended to make Reynard short-tempered and prone to lengthy diatribes about individual and corporate minimum taxes, the alternative minimum tax, and the antifamily implications of the marriage penalty instituted by the Tax Reform Act of 1969.

Nick's mother, Helena, spent much of his childhood running a struggling catering business; if the business cycle wasn't squeezing her, some city health inspector or rule triggered some other headache. The Bader family dinner table conversations were full of lamentations and fury over the tax code and federal, state, and city regulations of every kind, and they cultivated a righteous indignation in the son.

Perfect math SAT scores had gotten him into Princeton University with a brief Naval ROTC stint. He worked on the Hill until jumping on Reagan's bandwagon in 1976 and again in 1980. Now, he was not even thirty and working in the White House—or so he liked to say, even though technically he worked in the Old Executive Office Building.

Throughout the first weeks of the new administration, Bader prepared what he called Reagan's "naughty list" of government programs and agencies to be zeroed out in the upcoming year's budget proposal. A strange sense of honor and diligence drove him to look his foes in the eye as he broke the news. That sense of honor didn't go so far as to actually sympathize with the individuals whose jobs he aimed to eliminate; he considered most of the people before him to be parasites sucking on the national treasury. In a world where the Soviets were on the march in Afghanistan, the federal government was spending many times an average American's annual income on inane, pointless expenditures, such as $525,000 to convert 7 percent of the U.S. Coast Guard's personnel files to microfiche.[3]

Bader saw himself as righting the scales and unleashing a bit of holy wrath upon those who arrogantly assumed the American taxpayer would always pay whatever Washington demanded. He daydreamed of firing them all, but the civil service system made it nearly impossible to fire anyone, and removing

3   Editorial, "Fleeced Again," *Wilmington Morning Star*, April 24, 1980.

the threat of termination had a predictable impact on many government workers' sense of accountability and work ethic.

Joining the White House team made Bader feel slightly hypocritical, as he would have to fill out all the forms and become one of those government employees—albeit, he assured himself, temporarily. The public sector—roughly eighty-one million Americans, once you counted everyone receiving one form of public assistance or another—had to be paid for by the seventy million Americans working in the private sector.[4] Sure, government employees would quickly insist that they paid taxes too—but all of the money that constituted their salaries originally came from tax dollars taken from the private sector.

A government cannot raise money by taxing its own spending. All of the money has to come from somewhere else, and that somewhere else was either the private sector or borrowing. In this dilemma, Bader breathed slightly easier, knowing that as president, Reagan was going to draw a hard line on deficit spending.

When he contemplated the injustice of it all, and the callousness with which the federal bureaucracy greeted every April 16, Bader couldn't help but secretly feel a tinge of satisfaction at the tears and fury that greeted each meeting's bad news. One distraught EPA administrator had actually opened a window and stepped out onto the ledge, threatening to jump, after one meeting discussing cuts to environmental enforcement; Bader dealt with the potential brouhaha by circulating an internal memo outlining new security measures for windows and ledges.[5]

4   Ronald Reagan's radio commentary on "Government Cost," November 16, 1976. Whether or not these figures are accurate, Reagan (and a Reaganite like Bader) believed they were accurate.

5   A slight exaggeration; in 1982, the comic strip *Doonesbury* portrayed a distraught EPA official crawling out onto his ledge in protest of 'dismantling the whole

Today's meeting appeared particularly sweet to Bader: Somehow President Carter had been conned into creating a separate federal agency whose sole duty was monitoring and combating weeds. On paper, wiping this agency off the bureaucratic flowchart would be among his easiest and most satisfying. But breaking the news to Adam Humphrey would be a particularly delicious moment, as the small subculture of budget hawks on Capitol Hill had considered Humphrey to be a Svengali of appropriations fights. Bader knew a few bits of his background: Harvard undergrad, then Georgetown Law. He had been the legislative counsel to both House and Senate committees. His reputation was impressive but strangely vague—besides his negotiation skills, few knew much about him.

Bader smiled as he parked the car. Adam Humphrey and the Agency of Invasive Species would, too, bite the dust.

. . .

Bader awaited them in a conference room within the Old Executive Office Building. On his second day on the job, he had noticed that each leg of the chairs had an adjustable screw-peg at the bottom for balance, and had adjusted the chairs so that the ones on the visitors' side of the room were a quarter-inch shorter than the chairs on his side. Bader sat behind a conference table, flanked by two silent, stone-faced, square-jawed aides. He liked to think of them as the office assistant version of the Secret Service.

"Good morning, Mr. Bader!" Humphrey practically burst with good cheer upon entering the room. "Thank you so much

enforcement team.' Shortly thereafter, the real-life EPA administrator, Anne Gorsuch, issued a memo to all EPA employees protesting "windowsill politics."

for taking time out of your busy schedule to give us the opportunity to further illuminate the services this agency provides to the American people."

Bader didn't rise to greet him, but merely nodded.

"You can dispense with the pleasantries, Humphrey." He shot a sphincter-tightening smile at Wilkins and declared, "Sucking up to me isn't going to make me like your pathetic joke of an agency."

Humphrey's smile didn't budge. He gave a quick glance at Wilkins, as if to say, "See, right on schedule." He subtly made a fist and softly thumped his chest. Wilkins bit his tongue to avoid laughing as they sat down.

"Mr. Bader, you have no idea how difficult it has been to work here in Washington, within the federal workforce, and yearn for that new sheriff to establish that new order. Indeed, I was greatly reassured to see our new era of fiscal rectitude ushered in with the most expensive inauguration festivities in American history."

"Chalk that up to our predecessor's bang-up job on containing inflation," Bader snapped. "There's a new sheriff in town, and the attitude toward those who waste taxpayers' money is to hang 'em high."

Neither of Bader's aides had said a word after their terse introductions, but at this moment, for a split second, the one on the right pantomimed choking on a noose and smiled.

"We've got a lot of suspects to round up. Did you know this government spent more than a billion dollars on new furniture in the past ten years? At the same time, we've got seventy-eight—I counted—federally owned warehouses in the Washington area, storing piles upon piles of unused furniture, some wrapped in the original plastic."[6]

6 Associated Press, "Furniture Spending Questioned," March 18, 1980.

This was a monologue of righteous rage that Bader had rehearsed and performed in all of these meetings, and he enjoyed each one of them. He rose and strode to the window.

"You can see waste right outside this window. In July of 1979, they repaved the sidewalk outside the West Wing offices on the White House grounds. *Twice*. In one month!"[7]

He strode back to the table, walking behind Humphrey and Wilkins.

"That same year, the Justice Department estimated that one out of every ten federal dollars is wasted or stolen. We're talking *fifty billion dollars*, Humphrey. When the General Accounting Office set up a hotline to report all this waste and abuse, they received twenty-four hundred serious allegations in six weeks!" He consulted a memo before him. "Twenty-seven allegations of theft, twenty-two private uses of government property, seventy-two reports of employees not working a full workweek and fraudulently claiming that they did."[8]

Bader waited for Humphrey to squirm. Instead, Humphrey shook his head in sympathy of debatable sincerity.

"Mr. Bader, let me assure you I sympathize *deeply* with your effort to ensure waste and mismanagement are eliminated from the federal budget," Humphrey began. "No doubt, no agency is perfect, and I am sure that in the four years since our founding, the Agency for Invasive Species has made the occasional budgetary errors."

Bader sat and casually opened a file, readying his trap.

"Your agency opened up an office in Seattle and paid $100,000 for an abstract sculpture of rocks to adorn the entrance. A hundred grand for rocks, Humphrey! They cost $5.50

7   Frank Corimer, "Government Waste? Here Is a Perfect Example," Associated Press, July 19, 1979.

8   Associated Press, "Government Waste Described at Hearing," March 16, 1979.

per ton from the supply company. The artist spent less than fifty bucks on materials."[9]

"Oh, Mr. Bader, now you're reaching," Humphrey casually swatted away the argument. "The American government has many striking examples of art and architecture—the White House, the Capitol Dome . . . why, the very building we're in right now could be considered a piece of artwork. Is the Old Executive Office Building overpriced? Did the taxpayers get their money's worth when they paid Daniel Chester French to carve the statue of Lincoln within the Memorial? Who really can put a fair price on a piece of art?"

"Sotheby's," shot back Bader. He took another look at his file.

"Your agency helped create the new forms for pesticide manufacturers at the Environmental Protection Agency, correct?"

"Indeed, Mr. Bader, I consider the new report system an utter triumph of data collection, one that posterity will salute as a—"

"This is the report that must be submitted quarterly, that requires the second-quarter report to include a complete duplicate copy of the first-quarter report, the third-quarter report to include duplicate copies of the first and second quarters, and the fourth-quarter to include copies of the reports for the first three quarters? Reports that can run three thousand pages each?"

"That would be, I believe, an accurate summary of our method to reduce the cost to taxpayers of collating and coordinating quarterly reports, yes."

Bader had to chuckle at Humphrey's audacity, claiming that his Byzantine requirements were a cost-saving measure.

---

9   Actually, it was the General Services Administration under the Ford administration in 1975 that purchased a sculpture from Isamu Noguchi.

"Mr. Humphrey, right now in Afghanistan, some scrawny mujahedeen who hasn't eaten in three days is trying to fight off a Soviet battalion with a sharp stick. The Russian Bear is on the prowl in Central Asia, while the Arsenal of Democracy is spending billions to buy furniture that's collecting dust in some warehouse! Do you really think this administration should spend one more red cent on your little band of weed-pickers?"

Wilkins stifled a whimper. Humphrey stared back, coolly, and quietly drummed his fingers upon the conference room table.

"Very well, Mr. Bader. I just hope that if, indeed, the rumors are true, that the White House's upcoming budget proposal includes a plan to zero out this agency, that you account for our ongoing response to the Soviet-directed Halogeton infestation in the Western states, and see that it is not interrupted."

"The what?"

"You did get our latest updates on Moscow's continuing efforts to trigger an agricultural crisis, yes?"

"What?"

"Ah, that darn White House mail room. It seems your skepticism of the efficiencies of government has proven well-founded once again. Don't worry, I have a copy of our most recent updates here."

Bader furrowed his brow as Humphrey reached into his leather bag and dropped a stack of four binders, each three inches thick, onto the table, one by one. The covers were bright red and labeled:

USDA

AIS

RESPONSE TO SOVIET HALOGETON INFESTATION

CONFIDENTIAL, PLEASE

"As you no doubt know, Halogeton is a particularly nasty weed, deadly to livestock if consumed," Humphrey began, putting on his glasses and flipping through the report. Magnified ten thousand times, the plant appeared thorny, thick, and crooked, Godzilla in vegetative form.

"We have indeed traced its origin to the Soviet Union and China. A mere twenty-four ounces of Halogeton will kill a sheep within hours. One rancher in Idaho lost twelve thousand animals in one day."

Bader looked over his shoulder at his first aide, who offered a confused shrug. The other looked bug-eyed and mortified at his confusion.

"It is difficult to burn, requires little water to survive, and as a Republican congressman from Idaho accurately assessed, 'It would be a very fine thing to sabotage your enemy with.' The fact that the weed came from Soviet agents has been widely reported in the agricultural journals in the Western states, despite our efforts to keep a tight lid on this, lest the menace provoke a panic . . ."

Wilkins tried to suppress any facial expression, utterly bewildered by everything Humphrey was saying. He had been Humphrey's right-hand man for two years and had only the vaguest recollection of Halogeton. As Bader looked through the red-covered reports, he saw a wide variety of densely typed pages and maps with a hammer-and-sickle arriving in the Northwest and arrows spreading down through the Rockies. Bader left the report open to a grainy, black-and-white photo of Stalin laughing.

U.S. Department of Agriculture
Agency of Invasive Species

RESPONSE TO SOVIET HALOGETON INFESTATION

CONFIDENTIAL, PLEASE

Since the Communist Revolution, Soviet leaders have seethed at how the bounties of American agriculture put their farmers to shame. American farmers have one tractor for every 70 acres, their Soviet counterparts have one for every 485 acres. Starting in the 1930s, Soviet scientists have sought to devise new and insidious pests to unleash upon the American breadbasket and attack the Arsenal of Democracy through its vulnerable underbelly . . . our actual bellies.

Strains of Halogeton have been reported by American farmers for decades, but the USDA Agency of Invasive Species can say, with great certainty, that the increasing frequency and intensity of the infestation in recent years is the work of Soviet agents on American soil. (Literally.)

The Nature of the Threat

Halogeton is a weed that grows about 3 to 18 inches high, with spindly, needle-like leaves, like claws eager to grab all that is good and living and drag it to the salty earth below. Each small leaf has a sharp spine at its end that certain Agency of Invasive Species field investigators have nicknamed "Stalin's pitchfork."

Plants are green in the spring and early summer, then turn blood red or yellow by late summer. We believe the coloration may have been engineered by Soviet scientists to emulate the national flag.

The root system of the insidious invader helps bring salt to the surface, choking off most other plants. Thus, the vegetative villain is helping Moscow literally salt the earth of this great American nation.

Canada designated it a "noxious weed" in 1967.

Poisonous to horses, it can cause a neurological disease resembling Parkinson's.

Public Awareness

While the agency has, until this point, focused upon quiet, persistent efforts to contain and rebuke the ongoing Soviet biological warfare threat, there have been periodic reports revealing the threat to the public, particularly the agricultural community. It is our recommendation that the incoming administration tread carefully in discussing this topic.

Nonetheless, if skeptical minds within the administration need further confirmation of the breadth and depth of the threat that this agency alone is the vanguard against, we would refer you to several press accounts:

- The Journal of Range Management confirms, "Halogeton is a poisonous plant invader from the territory of the Soviet Union."

- The Associated Press reported Congress's appropriation to the Bureau of Land Management to "combat the spiny, barbed plant which was introduced from Russia. . . . The infestation has been costly. Where Halogeton grows, sheep die. In Idaho, 1,300 sheep in one flock died after eating the poisonous plant. . . . The latest BLM estimates list about 1,200,000 acres of public and private land now infested by the scourge of the range."

- The AP also reported, "SOVIET KILLER WEED INVADES CALIFORNIA," breaking news of a "mysterious" arrival of the weed native to the Ukraine. That report noted that the weed can kill sheep within hours of consumption. Only swift action by the Agency of Invasive Species contained and eliminated that outbreak.

- Another columnist let slip that the weed "could threaten us with starvation" and

"Communist agents are sprinkling Halogeton seed." A Republican congressman leaked to that columnist, "It would be a very fine thing to sabotage your enemies with."

While these reports document the threat in sufficient detail to dissuade the most stubborn skeptic, the sort of fellow who never questions where his food comes from, or spends much time thinking about the long-term safety of American agriculture or food supply, we would urge the administration to refrain from greater public discussion of the Halogeton threat. Among certain employees of the Agency of Invasive Species, there is a saying: "The best way to uproot is to remain publicly mute." The recommendation for secrecy is based upon the following:

The Soviet Intent

While the senior staff of the Agency of Invasive Species realizes that our role is to enact policy, not to make policy, we would recommend lawmakers immediately consider an increase of funding but minimal discussion of the threat. If the Soviet Halogeton threat were to be discussed in the nation's major newspapers or the nightly newscasts, one could easily see a panic and hoarding of food. Having witnessed the economic chaos brought about by spiking gasoline prices in recent years, one can only conclude that a panic about wheat and other grain prices would only be exponentially worse, with perhaps a breakdown in law and order in portions of the country with food shortages. Our senior analysts note, with some trepidation, that the Washington D.C. area would likely be among the first to experience food shortages if, indeed, a panic started after the revelation of the Soviet Halogeton threat. The paralysis of the nation's capital from food riots might be the trigger for Soviets' final strike against the leader of the free world.

Again, we emphasize that as public servants,

our role is merely to implement the policy of much wiser minds in the administration and Congress. But our analysis of the dangerous circumstances leads us to recommend a modest increase of funding of sixty (60) percent, under the cover of "increased administrative services." The agency would then be able to dramatically increase its Halogeton mitigation operations.

ABOVE: We believe this painting, hanging in the lobby of the Soviet Ministry of Agriculture in Moscow, depicts Stalin distributing Halogeton to children who are in fact USSR sleeper agents on their way to America.

Humphrey flipped open to an artist's depiction of a herd of wild mustangs, all dying in the sun. A cowboy who could be easily mistaken for the Marlboro Man was holding his hat over his heart, a single tear running down his cheek. In the corner of the illustration, the crooked lines of the perhaps excessively anthropomorphized weed seemed to be almost smiling.

"The weed is particularly dangerous to horses. I'm sure the president knows this, being a rancher and all . . . I need not remind you that we share the president's distinctive appreciation for the Equine-American Community. The manifestation is currently most prevalent in the Mountain states, but is inching its way to California—I fear an interruption in funding would lead to odious crimson and yellow Halogeton sprigs cropping up all over the Golden State . . . and while it is far from my role to set national policy, speaking personally I for one would find that an unacceptable risk to Little Man."

Bader had a hard time tearing his eyes away from the vivid apocalyptic depiction of the stallion massacre, and it took a moment for him to catch up to Humphrey's flourish to drive the point home.

"Little Man? Wait, you mean—"

Humphrey revealed his first well-rehearsed flickers of irritation and impatience. "President Reagan's *horse*, Mr. Bader. His black colt bred from Baby, the gray thoroughbred stallion he received during his Hollywood years. Currently resides at the president's ranch. You do know the man you work for, don't you, Mr. Bader? I was informed you are the president's right hand? That profile in *Time* called you '*Reagan's bloody right hand*'?"

Bader and his unspeaking aides seemed to communicate entirely through glances.

> First glance, from Bader: *Why am I just learning of this now?*
>
> Second glance, from the aides: *What are you looking at us for? We're just learning of this now!*
>
> Third glance, from Bader: *What are you paid for?*
>
> Fourth glance, from the aides: *Don't blame us, he said it was the White House mail room!*

If the glances and glares of disapproval and recrimination grew any more intense, eyeballs would start popping out of their sockets.

Finally, Bader sighed.

"I'll level with you, Humphrey, AIS was top of my list for cuts, but in light of this, I'm going to have to reevaluate our recommendation about your agency," Bader said, rubbing his forehead. "This is big.

"God, Moscow's been trying to choke us off, right under our noses . . ." Bader took one last flip through the book, then looked up at Humphrey. "I can't promise anything, but I think we're going to have to see if we can get you guys some of the DOD funding we'll be pushing on the Hill."

Wilkins noticed that Humphrey reacted with a much bigger grin than the smile in his wedding photo on his desk.

. . .

Wilkins waited until they were in the cab before letting out any reaction to the meeting's unexpected turn of events, then burst forth with an explosion of giddy laughter. Humphrey merely beamed, looking out the window.

"How the hell did you do that?!" Wilkins yipped excitedly. "Bader never wants to spend more money! I nearly peed myself when he said he would make the pitch to Weinberger on the way out. How did you find all of that stuff on the Soviets? I mean, it's unbelievable!" As soon as Wilkins finished the final word, he had a sudden, horrific realization. "I mean, really unbelievable . . . Really, really, *really* unbelievable. I mean, as in, I'm starting to think that everything you said is something that cannot be believed."

"Of course not, Mr. Wilkins, breathe easy," Humphrey chuckled. "Everything within the report is accurate . . . *technically*. Some of the sourcing is from the 1950s, when concerns and suspicions about Soviet activity on American soil were . . . perhaps excessive."

"Which ones?"

"Oh, the 'Soviet Killer Weed' headline was from 1950, the public range estimates were from 1951, around then ... the Republican congressman's comment was from 1952, I believe."

Wilkins winced. "Adam, has anyone turned up any evidence of this vast Russian plot in, say, the past thirty years?"

"The *broad outlines* of the report are accurate; Halogeton is a menace, our job is to fight it. It is widely believed to be the work of the Soviets, and increasing our budget would only serve the best interest of the American people."

"So you just bet our jobs and our pensions on the White House believing a reheated pile of Red Scare propaganda?"

"People have always attributed vegetative and insect pests to the sinister work of their enemies. In past cultures, it was attributed to omens and curses and spells and other magic. Today we fear what comes out of the laboratory. In decades past, Dakotans called the tumbleweed 'the Russian weed.' Long Island fishermen in the 1950s called a newly arrived seaweed 'Sputnik Weed,' believing that Soviet spacecraft had spread it."

"How do you know all this stuff?" Wilkins asked.

"A healthy agency does not require relevance to the national agenda so much as the *appearance* of relevance to the national agenda," Humphrey explained. "It is perhaps the second-most important tool in ensuring continued funding."

"And the most important?"

"A friend on the Appropriations Committee."

The cab took them to Capitol Hill, where Humphrey had his second important meeting of the day, to meet a long-serving congressman from the Bluegrass State.

The Washington Post

A24   August 13, 1980

Pork, Personified

By Rowland Evans and Robert Novak

WASHINGTON—Last month a national newsweekly called Rep. Vernon Hargis, D-Ky., "the most important man in Washington you've never heard of." The profile offered a glowing spin to what is an increasingly common practice in Congress: egregiously corrupt horse-trading of votes for expensive projects called 'earmarks.'

Kentucky's Seventh Congressional District represents a cluster of the state's poorest counties, a stretch of Appalachia along the West Virginia border. In 1956, the district elected Hargis, a local lawyer who had seen hell in Korea and rarely hesitates to remind anyone of it. (He invokes his "dodging the bullets of hordes of d—ned Chinamen" stories reflexively whenever anyone dares bring up what he once euphemistically called his "purely recreational" attendance at a Ku Klux Klan cross burning in his youth.)

Early in his congressional career, Hargis saw the power of the purse and committed himself, with a ruthlessness his peers label "obsessive," to getting a seat on the Appropriations Committee. In his second term he was selected to join the powerful panel that controlled spending and immediately became one of the House's consummate dealmakers. Determined to never leave his perch, he has proven willing to add just about anything to an appropriations bill, provided the favor was returned.

As a result, Kentucky's Seventh Congressional District, which consists mostly of small towns tucked among the Appalachian mountains, now hosts regional offices (and jobs) of:

- The U.S. Department of Commerce
- The U.S. Department of Interior
- The U.S. Department of Health and Human Services

- The U.S. Department of Labor
- The U.S. Equal Employment Opportunity Commission
- The U.S. Small Business Administration
- Two U.S. Fish and Wildlife Service facilities, including an aquarium and marine life facility
- The U.S. Census Bureau
- The Environmental Protection Agency
- The Department of Agriculture's Agency of Invasive Species (two, in fact)

In addition, the district also houses:

- a NORAD tracking facility
- a research center for NASA
- a Department of Defense heliport
- a Department of Transportation vehicle safety research center
- a Department of Energy Cold Fusion Research Laboratory
- a federally funded aerospace technology center, freeway, federal courthouse, an industrial park, an education research institute, several historical parks, rural health centers, four dams, an exceptionally well-funded branch of the state university and several community colleges, and a gold-plated medical center (with remarkably few patients)

Almost all of these, of course, are named after Hargis. None of the spokesmen for any of these departments or agencies would give an explanation, on the record, of why this rural Kentucky district was chosen for their branch offices.

One agency spokesman, requesting anonymity, explained simply, "He's on the Appropriations Committee, what can we do?"

For weeks, Hargis refused several requests for comment on these district projects; finally, his office issued a written statement that "Congressman Hargis is proud of his service for the people of his district, and will never forget that his job is to serve the simple people who built this country, who fought and bled and died for this country."

Reached in the halls of Congress, Hargis sped away after dismissing the inquiry as "a city slicker reporter in fancy shoes."

Criticism of Hargis's free-spending ways is unlikely to matter; decades of increasingly-precise redistricting have given Hargis an airtight political lock on his district. Kentucky Republicans haven't even run a candidate against Hargis since 1972, when one Floyd Robbs, a town councilman from Turner's Grove, garnered 20 percent of the vote. One official with the state GOP noted that in the gushing river of federal funds that flowed from Washington to the district in the past eight years, not one cent has ever gone to the county that includes Turner's Grove.

"The congressman has a long memory," the party member lamented.

In just three years, the Agency of Invasive Species had established *two* regional offices in Hargis's district, even though the amount of agriculture in the region was measured less in acres than in backyards. Only Siamese twins had a relationship more symbiotic than that of Adam Humphrey and Vernon Hargis.

"Mr. Chairm—ah, Congressman, I find myself too eager to promote you!" Humphrey greeted the congressman after a forty-minute wait in his office lobby.

"Ah, Humph, I don't need that trouble," said Hargis, slapping his back. The congressman was the only man who called the director "Humph," a nickname that he detested, but Humphrey greeted the appellation and the bruise-inducing backslap with a perfect façade of warm admiration.

Wilkins was introduced to the congressman for the sixth time, with Hargis showing no flicker of recognition. The pictures of the young congressman on the wall featured a slick, skinny, hungry-eyed man on a mission. The past twenty years had added thirty pounds and several chins, and the hair had shifted from black to silver.

"After discussion with the White House, I believe the

administration has found some value in our efforts to combat the scourge of Halogeton, and may see a national security interest in assigning more funds to that effort," Humphrey said, with a carefully calibrated expression of enthusiasm.

"These guys?" Hargis's eyebrows popped up. "You must have given them some song and dance, Humph."

"Oh, you flatter me, Congressman," said Humphrey, mugging humility. "I merely laid out the dire implications of delay on this matter, and how this particular threat to American agriculture required all deliberate speed."

Wilkins couldn't help himself. "You could say, now they're *Russian* to find more money for it!" Humphrey shot Wilkins a silencing glare.

"Anyway, Mr. Ch—er, Congressman, I was hoping you could push through a boost in our funding." Humphrey turned over a much shorter memo than the mountain of documents he used to strafe Bader. "You'll find my recommended figures here, and on this sheet, you'll see a more specific proposal. I was thinking that the community of Gail Bluff would make a fine location for a new AIS Halogeton Management Research Center."

Wilkins had a hand in this part of the proposal; his job was to find the largest town in Hargis's district that had not yet had any federal facility in it. The task was surprisingly difficult.

"Humphrey, you just make my day every time you come up here," Hargis said with an approving nod. "I was just thinking about what I could do for all the poor folk in Gail Bluff looking for work—practically half the town's on public assistance."

I understand it's a largely moonshine-based economy, Wilkins thought to himself. He opened his mouth to speak, but another look from Humphrey said simply: *Shut it*.

"I think there's a darn good chance I can make this happen," Hargis nodded, scribbling a note on the margin of the memo. "It'll take some horse trading, but building coalitions is what I do. I'll tie this to some city spending—food stamps or something—and I'll get the rurals and the urbans together, and everybody wins!"

The men rose, and vigorous handshakes ensued.

"Congressman, may you live to be a hundred, and serve the rest of your days!"

"Humph, you know the only way I'll ever leave this office is in a pine box," Hargis laughed.

. . .

The additional funding for the Agency of Invasive Species sailed through smoothly, and Nicholas Bader's attention turned to other departments and agencies. However, it didn't take long for his spending-cut crusade to get stymied, and he began to think of the morning meeting with Humphrey as a critical misstep in his mission for budgetary discipline.

One month after the meeting, President Reagan was shot. Thankfully, he survived. But those who knew the president said he was a different man afterward, less energetic but clearer in his priorities, more focused on the Soviet threat and less focused on cutting the federal government where possible.

About a year into Reagan's first term, OMB Director David Stockman went rogue, telling *The Atlantic* magazine that the president's budget proposal included "snap judgments" and unnervingly confessing, "None of us really understands what's going on with all these numbers." He discussed using "magic asterisks" to make budgets appear more balanced by assuming additional unspecified cuts in the future. He complained that the president backed down on some of the biggest and boldest cuts and barely understood the decisions he was making. He painted a picture of an administration, bit by bit, making its peace with special interest politics and abandoning the dream of a dramatically scaled-back government unleashing the entrepreneurial spirit of Americans. Most administrations had at least one disgruntled staffer who aired all the dirty laundry, but Stockman did the unthinkable: He did it all on the record.

While Stockman remained at OMB, he quickly became regarded with suspicion and ridicule among the rest of the Reaganites. Bader was mortified to find that the reckless mouth of the man he once considered a rival had somehow tainted the good name of all the administration's budgetary ax men, and the budget hawks found themselves torn by internal divisions. Bit by bit, cutting costs slid down the list of priorities. Bader found that for a lot of his fellow Reaganites, deficit spending represented an acceptable short-term tool to finance increased defense spending and much-needed tax cuts.

Two years later, after repeatedly pestering the Central Intelligence Agency for a briefing on the subject, Bader eventually learned that the Halogeton problem in the Western states was, in all likelihood, a natural occurrence and not deliberate Soviet sabotage. But by then, the increased infusion of cash from the 1981 budget proposal was now part of the baseline for the agency's annual funding level. Humiliated, Bader did what he could to erase any record of him touting the AIS effort against the Soviets.

Month by month, Bader found himself increasingly on the outside of the administration's inner circle. He wasn't invited to the same meetings, phone calls went unreturned, memos missed him, he learned of administration decisions in the *Washington Post*. He expected to find himself the target of leaks in the *Post* and other publications, but sadly realized he was below the threshold of political relevance; he, his decisions, and his work simply weren't important enough to leak about anymore.

In 1984, Bader left the White House and joined the Washington office of a private investment firm.

* * *

MARCH 1985
U.S. National Debt: $1.7 trillion
Budget, USDA Agency of Invasive Species: $45.4 million

Now earning good money in the private sector, Bader took his wife for an anniversary dinner at the restaurant atop the Kennedy Center.

On the car radio on the way there, a Norwegian trio urged listeners to embrace the potential confrontation, as the singer would be gone in a day or two. They parked and strode to the massive performance hall, enjoying the first warm night of spring. Bader knew he was supposed to be celebratory, but looking down the Mall at the Capitol Dome, just beyond the Washington Monument, reminded him of his task unfinished. He was making gobs of money now, but he still had that seething fury every spring as tax season approached.

His mood turned significantly worse when he entered the dining room and saw Humphrey, Mr. Halogeton Menace himself, finishing his meal. After the host brought Bader and his wife to their table, he excused himself and immediately began hunting Humphrey.

A moment later, he found him, standing upon the terrace, looking out at the Mall.

"Hey, Humphrey! Run into any Soviet spies in those cornfields lately?" Bader sneered.

"Come again?" Humphrey instantly recognized Bader, but

feigned not remembering him for a few seconds. "Ah, yes, Mr. Bader! Formerly of the White House! How are things?"

Bader scowled. "I should have known everything you would say was absolute horsesh—"

"Mr. Bader, as I recall, everything I told you represented the very best information we had at the time. Don't tell me that the intervening years have made you . . . less vigilant about the Soviet threat."

Bader stepped forward, and for a moment, the patrons who noticed their tense exchange thought Bader would knock Humphrey's teeth down his throat. But instead he merely jabbed a finger into Humphrey's sternum with striking force.

"You humiliated me, Humphrey. I trusted you, you manipulated me, and I looked like a fool because of you! You tricked me into approving taxpayer money getting shoveled down that rat hole of yours! Nobody plays me for a fool."

Humphrey couldn't help himself. "You can't say no one does something immediately after you declare that I have done that precise act."

The veins in Bader's neck bulged. "I will make you pay."

"Oh, Nicholas . . ." Humphrey slowly backed away. "There's no need to take a budgetary disagreement so personally."

"I'm serious, Humphrey. I don't care if it takes years: Someday I'm going to cut the budget for your agency to a great . . . big . . . zero."

He stormed off. Humphrey chuckled, concluding that Nick Bader was more likely to sprout wings than to make good on his threat.

2

Agency of Invasive Species Administrative Director Adam Humphrey told his assistant Jack Wilkins about his run-in with Bader, and Wilkins laughed. He couldn't believe how much he had once feared Bader. He chuckled about how little he knew when he came to work for Humphrey; all he really remembered was that he was desperate to get away from what he thought would be his dream job, working in the White House.

OCTOBER 1979
U.S. National Debt: $826 billion
Budget, USDA Agency of Invasive Species: $13.4 million

Wilkins had spent three years working as the lowest-paid, least-senior staff researcher in the Carter administration. His friends told him he looked like he aged a decade in that time. White House work had that effect on people, particularly among those too junior to really change anything, but still senior enough to get yelled at and to feel emotionally invested in the performance of the administration.

The trouble had started early. First Tip O'Neill threw a fit when his tickets to the Inaugural Gala at the Kennedy Center had been in the back row of the balcony, and had later complained about the skimpy continental breakfasts at White House meetings.[10] The late 1970s turned into a blur of presidential disasters: Managing the tennis courts. Sweaters. Letters and phone calls unreturned. Throw in 18 percent inflation and gas lines. Now everyone at the White House was screaming about whether they should let the Shah of Iran come to the Mayo Clinic, as if letting a man seek a treatment for his cancer could somehow be a bad thing. Wilkins had sensed the need to push the ejector button and get out of politics and get into something quieter, safer, more stable and predictable. He decided he needed a safe job in the civil service.

Wilkins heard the administrative director in some obscure federal agency was looking for a new right-hand man—and so he ended up sitting before the desk of Adam Humphrey, Administrative Director, Department of Agriculture's Agency of Invasive Species, serving under the Bureau of Agricultural Risk Management, under the Undersecretary of Farm Services, under the Deputy Secretary of Agriculture, under the Secretary of Agriculture.

The president appointed and the Senate confirmed the agency's director—currently some congressman who desperately sought, and found, an excuse to avoid the judgment of his district's disgruntled voters—but Humphrey was the real power.

"So why do you want to leave that most glamorous of workplaces, the White House, and come work at a place like the Agency of Invasive Species?"

"I want to serve my country in the civil service."

"Very good, Mr. Wilkins, your utterly predictable textbook answer will be noted. So what's the *real* reason?"

---

10 John A. Farrell, *Tip O'Neill and the Democratic Century*, Little, Brown and Company, 2001.

Wilkins stared for a moment, sighed, and figured he might as well reveal it all to see if his potential new boss sympathized.

"I've now had my heart broken twice," he said, glancing out the window. "First as a volunteer for Teens for McGovern when he lost, then by Carter when he won. I figure there's a 50-50 shot I may lose my White House job next January. Campaign work means long hours, candidates that forget to pay you, and low pay even when they remember, sleeping on the couch in the office and watching your candidate blow it all by saying he's undecided on whether kids should start the day by reciting the Pledge of Allegiance. The Hill isn't much better, and every two years your boss can get fired by fickle hicks who decide they like some smooth-talking local car salesman better—and that's presuming he doesn't get caught jumping into the Tidal Basin with a stripper."

Wilkins watched Humphrey's face for any sign of disapproval, but he simply saw a serene smile staring back at him.

"Plus, my girlfriend wants me to marry her, and I figure that means I need a steadier job. Regular hours, weekends off, less craziness, less stress."

Humphrey's smile turned into a chuckle and he put his fingertips together. "Ah, the civilizing influence of women." He picked up Wilkins's resume.

"Mr. Wilkins, your resume and references excited all of the right personnel people—such dedication to public service! Such a spirited drive to every task before you! But I saw a warning sign or two. I feared you might be some upstart, hell-bent on turning everything upside down in an impatient crusade to achieve your theoretical ideal overnight. As you no doubt saw at the White House, the wheels of government turn slowly. Deliberately. I envision great things for the future of this agency, but at a careful and measured pace! I prefer to consolidate our gains and carefully and methodically manage our steady growth and progress. Cabinet secretaries and agency directors come and go every few years. Comparably, we are eternal."

Wilkins smiled at the audacious boast.

"If the young lady in your life desires you to be in steady work, we will fit that bill."

. . .

Wilkins settled in within a few weeks.

Many of the mornings began with Wilkins keeping up with Humphrey's deliberate stride through the labyrinthine halls of the Department of Agriculture.

"We're lucky to work in this building," Humphrey said thoughtfully. "We're the only federal department on the national mall. More tourists see us, by accident, than the Pentagon or the State Department or any other cabinet department."

"I feel like these hallways go on forever," Wilkins said.

The Department of Agriculture's headquarters actually uses up two massive buildings, the Administrative Building on the north side of Independence Avenue and the South Building, connected with two arched pedestrian bridges. Employees rarely if ever use them. The South Building is seven stories and includes 4,500 rooms in a precise grid; only the departmental auditorium and library interrupt the dizzying pattern. With floors, hallways, and closed office doors all looking the same, Wilkins found himself getting turned around and lost with surprising frequency.

"This was, until the Pentagon was completed, the largest office building in the world. Congress decreed that no building in the city could be taller than the Capitol—a rule, I suspect, designed to remind everyone where the power and the money was," Humphrey explained. "Washington never had skyscrapers, and I suspect that shapes the way we work. Had the federal workforce been housed in giant towers, well . . . our office culture might have evolved like the ones of Wall Street banks or publishing houses. But instead of connecting our offices vertically we're connected horizontally, and it creates a certain . . ."

"Inefficiency?" Wilkins guessed, noticing that he was wearing through the soles of his dress shoes in the new job.

"Geographic ambiguity."

They turned a corner. "As you know, we have a new director."

"I've been reading up on him," Wilkins declared, hoping for approval.

"Most presidential appointees are being rewarded for years of loyal party service," began Humphrey in one of his monologues of How Washington Works.

"The Secretary of Agriculture always goes to some farm-state senator or governor or member of Congress. Presidents seem to think the primary qualification for the position is the ability to deliver a win in the Iowa caucus. The undersecretary slots often go to lesser friends and figures. A directorship is something of a snub, really. Our former director had been hoping for an ambassadorship to one of those Western European countries with rich food and women with high cheekbones. But our new one, like our first, is a former lawmaker, this one a longtime ally of the president from his time in Georgia. There are many advantages to having former legislators in the role of agency director."

"They bring good relationships with the Hill with them?"

"Mmm, not what I had in mind. It's more that they rarely have run very much beyond their congressional office, and thus have little sense of how to handle a large and complicated organization. Any new appointee spends his first months figuring out how everything works, and by that point, their interest in mucking around with things is . . . worn away by the sands of time. If we want something, we tell him we need it, and he will approve it. If we don't want something, we tell him it will be impossible to implement, and he will move on. In time, even the strongest-willed appointee can be conditioned to accept our helpful guidance."

Wilkins sensed something slightly Orwellian about the term "conditioned," but nodded and waited.

"Information management is one of the keys. Ideally, our director, the secretary, and the deputy secretaries will be kept hermetically sealed from all potentially troublesome 'flows' of information. We screen the calls, sort out the letters, divert the unnecessary memos. Our management's time is exceptionally valuable and one of our key duties is ensuring that none of their time is wasted by reading or hearing anything that we do not find productive. The old policy was that no one could see the AIS director without a scheduled appointment except the secretary, the undersecretary, myself, my assistant, the director's personal secretary, and the director's wife. Under the new policy, wives must call ahead."

"I'm not even going to ask why."

"Good instincts, Mr. Wilkins. With a new director, I like to hit the ground running and schedule appointments from 7:15 breakfast meetings to evening dinner receptions ending at 9:00 p.m."

He handed Wilkins a typewritten form:

7:30: Preparatory meeting, Director, Director's personal staff, Administrative Director

7:45: Breakfast meeting with Kansas State Chapter of National 4-H

8:15: Address, opening session of Mid-Atlantic Farmers Union convention

9:00: Senior Staff Meeting, USDA Conference Room

10:00: Meeting, Secretary of Agriculture

10:30: Staff briefing on competitiveness trends among pesticide producers internationally

10:45: Rapid review of morning paperwork

11:00: Policy coordination meeting with management, U.S. Fish and Wildlife Service

11:30: Luncheon, Society for Pesticide Reduction & Agricultural Yields (SPRAY)

12:45: Arrive second luncheon, U.S. House of Representatives Wheat Caucus

1:45: Meeting with Mr. N. Naylor, Academy for Tobacco Studies

2:30: Briefing to review pending publication, *Yellow Starthistle: The Creeping Menace Under Our Feet*

3:30: Meeting, National Association to Stamp Out Fire Ants

4:00: Security briefing with N. Solo, the man from United Network Command for Law and Enforcement

4:20: Meeting, update on activities of branch offices

4:30: Creative-Problem-Solving Presentation from Department of External Services

5:00: Phone call, National Corn Growers Association

5:30: Potential review, preparation for following day's agenda

5:45: Change to black tie

6:00: Cocktail reception, Washington Hilton, Mid-Atlantic Farmers Union Maryland Delegation

6:30–8:00: banquet, Mid-Atlantic Farmers Union

Wilkins whistled. "This looks exhausting."
"Precisely the point, Mr. Wilkins," Humphrey replied.

"Within weeks, the director is begging for the schedule to be lightened and I comply with the request by dramatically lessening it—one morning meeting, one afternoon evening, and letting him know everything that needs his approval or consent is done by 3:00 p.m. I try to have nothing scheduled for Fridays."

"That seems a little light."

"It's best for all involved. He dare not request a busier schedule, having nearly collapsed under the initial marathon. Eventually he will withdraw from the decision-making loop entirely."

"I notice most meals end up with two meetings around them."

"The average director gains twenty pounds during his tenure."

They turned another corner.

"You will notice the director is constantly escorted by at least two staffers—we need a backup unless he gets separated. He is driven everywhere, and the advance team ensures he spends no more time at any particular meeting than needed. Quickly in, quickly out. No dilly-dallying."

"I get it. One delay in the morning can set back the whole day."

"That, and again, we don't want him talking to anyone if we can help it. If he talks to people, he might listen to them, and if he listens to them, there's no telling what ideas might end up in his head. That's why the best and most efficient way for the agency to operate is for us to carefully manage the schedule, what gets briefed to him, and so on. We need to ensure that the director's time and energy are not wasted by extraneous matters. Otherwise he would be deluged with meetings, calls, letters, demands."

"How do we make sure he hears what he needs to hear?"

Humphrey couldn't quite stifle a chuckle. "Your question

presupposes that an agency director cares to hear anything from anyone besides himself. But when we get a particularly curious one, I find it useful to ensure he is deluged with data that confirms his preconceptions. He needs to conclude that he knows all there is to know and to accept the recommendations given to him. I find 'placidity' a goal to encourage in agency management. Think of it as 'strategic disengagement.'"

They turned another corner, and Wilkins momentarily wondered if Humphrey had just absentmindedly led him in a circle. "And you can't watch directors too closely," Humphrey warned. "Early on, our last one walked out of his office and was lost for an hour. I had security retrieve him. They found him in the print shop, learning from some GS-7 how the equipment worked. I told him that wandering off like that was very unsafe."

Often Wilkins wondered if Humphrey was pulling his leg, but there had been no overt signs that Humphrey was a deliberate prankster. "Unsafe? This is the Department of Agriculture, not Afghanistan."

Humphrey's placid exterior hid his willingness to tease. "Really, Mr. Wilkins? Am I to understand that a veteran of the Carter White House is implying the inquiry, 'what could possibly go wrong?'"

· · ·

Wilkins learned to like working for Humphrey.

Sure, Humphrey could be stuffy, arrogant, and an insufferable snob, but he was also an eager teacher, a treasure trove of information in the workings of government, and an insightful student of human psychology. He was the oldest of old school in style but adaptable to any challenge the world threw at him and utterly unflappable in dealing with whatever problem bedeviled the agency on any given day. He could even, on the occasional night after a drink or two, be funny.

Humphrey's marriage remained a mystery to Wilkins. He had met Humphrey's wife, Dolores, at the office Christmas party, and she seemed a pleasant enough woman who worked as a hospital administrator. Wilkins would periodically ask how she was, and his boss would give generic pleasant answers. The more Wilkins observed Humphrey's reticence to talk about his wife, the more he suspected something wasn't well.

The couple had no children so far and Humphrey never suggested that some might arrive someday. At the second Christmas party, in 1980, a procurement contract analyst was met in the office by his wife and their brood of five kids. Wilkins noticed that neither Humphrey nor Dolores warmed at the sight of them, and in fact Humphrey's wife seemed to avoid them. Wilkins wondered if one or both were infertile, and sensed that the pair channeled the energies usually devoted to making a family into their jobs.

Periodically, Wilkins got the impression that Humphrey's interest in life outside government and politics was merely studying the role for the appropriate small talk needed to grease the wheels of his professional life: *"How about those Redskins?"* . . . *"No, I haven't seen* Apocalypse Now, *but everyone who does see it either loves it or hates it."* . . . *"I just feel so bad for all those athletes who have trained so hard and who won't go to Moscow for the Olympics."*

Humphrey's true passion was work, and Wilkins found him to be an unparalleled mentor. He taught Wilkins to thrive using the oldest and most basic equipment; upgrades were rare, held up by a Byzantine procurement process, and every transaction had to be checked and double-checked for security risks and contractor quality assurance and a million other reasons that sounded good in theory but proved nearly unworkable in practice. The purchase of one fifteen-page guide for a word processor required the supplier to fill out seventeen pages of forms.[11]

Humphrey also taught Wilkins to never fire anyone; only to transfer them. To fire someone was to risk a lawsuit, and in many cases, the federal government had already spent some considerable sum to train them. Besides the hassle of actually removing a name from the payroll and all of the associated paperwork, Humphrey considered an unfilled job a sin; his aim was to have as few empty slots as possible.

"If a job is unfilled, someone might get the idea that it's not necessary," Humphrey lectured on more than one occasion.

Perhaps most importantly, Humphrey believed in never leaving a dollar unspent. Humphrey rarely lost his temper, but unused account funds at the end of the fiscal year were the one time you could count on an eye-bulging, vein-throbbing tirade.

"If we have money left in our budget at the end of the year, the Powers That Be will conclude we don't need as much in the next year's budget," he emphasized, time and again. "To achieve our mission, we need more resources. Always. Forever. Never let anyone hear that we have enough money to meet our goals."

Not only was Humphrey masterful at persuading Congress to send ever-larger sums to the agency, but he managed to siphon off bits and pieces from other portions of the federal budget. In an early conversation, Humphrey revealed, "Through our interagency working group, portions of our funding come from partnerships with the Departments of Agriculture, Commerce, Interior, Defense, Treasury, HHS, the U.S. Trade

---

11 Slight exaggeration, but only slight: A book purchase in the Chicago public school system requires seventeen pages of forms to be filled out by the publisher.

Representative, EPA, Secretary of State, USAID, Transportation, and NASA."[12]

"NASA?" Wilkins asked incredulously. "What, are we on the lookout for killer weeds from outer space?"

APRIL 1983

U.S. National Debt: $1.34 trillion

Budget, USDA Agency of Invasive Species: $39.6 million

It only took about four years of working side by side for Wilkins to feel like he had finally decoded Humphrey.

The breakthrough arrived one Friday night after the two had dinner with their wives at Wilkins's house in Takoma Park.

Dolores and Wilkins's wife, Candice, had retired to the other room, teasing their husbands that the shop talk had become unbearable. The work talk had abated a bit, and the two men were half-watching a television where David Copperfield pledged to make the Statue of Liberty disappear.

Wilkins asked a question that had been nagging at him for years. "So how did you end up at the agency, Adam?" Late at night, and after many drinks, Wilkins felt bold enough to use his first name. "You're the smartest man I know. You could do anything. Why are you an administrative director of a federal agency most people have never heard of?"

Humphrey stared at the television screen, where Copperfield continued to promise the impossible.

"You think I'm a magician, don't you, Jack?" he said with a not-entirely-sober giggle.

"I've seen you run rings around guys who want pieces of our

---

12 All of these agencies are in fact part of the National Invasive Species Council, the real-life inspiration for the Agency of Invasive Species.

budget, and they come out of the meeting convinced that giving us more was their idea all along," Wilkins said with raised eyebrows. "So, yeah, I'd like you to teach me that Jedi mind-trick someday!"

"Genetics, I suppose," Humphrey said, triggering a puzzled expression from Wilkins. "My father was, in his time, perhaps the best car salesman in New England. For a while, at least. Studebakers. Then he moved on to running advertising campaigns for the dealers in the area and across the state—television, radio, newspaper, print advertising, the works. He was quite good at it. A master, really. Understood people inside and out. It's not that he taught me everything I know, but he certainly set me on the path of studying how people think, how they make decisions, how to . . . nudge them in the direction you would prefer."

"So why aren't you selling cars? I can see you out on the lot, saying, 'Just get behind the wheel of this all-new Chevrolet Caprice Classic.'"

Humphrey smiled. "My junior year of high school, I was on track to be valedictorian. All set to apply to Harvard. Brightest future ahead. One day, I come home from school and my father tells me he has bad news. He's been laid off, but . . . things will be okay."

Humphrey's smile disappeared. "The cars weren't selling. My father didn't make the cars, he didn't price them; his job was to get people into the dealerships and he did that—as well as anyone. And they let him go anyway.

"He's certain he'll find work again soon, but the family has bills to pay. We try to act like everything's normal, but month by month, the money is getting tighter. My parents tried to hide it, but it was obvious. Senior year, I apply to Harvard . . . and I'm accepted! But when I tell my parents . . . they look heartbroken instead of elated."

Wilkins exhaled with sympathy.

"It should have been one of the happiest moments of my life—and it's all ruined by the fact that they're terrified they won't be able to afford it. The financial aid system wasn't as well organized or generous then—most Ivy League students were from families making, oh, probably at least twice the national median income, and we were scraping along on savings. Anyway, the short version is that come next fall, all of my friends and classmates are going off to other colleges—and I'm spending a year working for the local parks department. And yes, weed management was one of my duties."

"Urgh. But you ended up at Harvard, so things turned out okay." Wilkins tried to remain cheery.

"Yes, but I had a whole year to contemplate the faceless, unknown middle-management budget-cutter who deemed my father extraneous, and who turned my bright future upside down," Humphrey fumed. " 'What's good for General Motors is good for America'—HA! Wilkins, every day in this country, somebody loses their job for no fault of their own. Sometimes it's a mass layoff, sometimes it's just one person, but the effect is the same on the poor soul deemed expendable: no sense of where their next paycheck is coming from, just, 'Thank you for your service, clean out your desk, see you, goodbye.' Eventually Dad found another job and did all right. But I knew then I would never end up selling cars, or working for some fool in an executive suite who might toss me out to save his quarterly earnings report. No, I would go into government."

"I know that feeling. Change the world. Make it a better place. Still, most folks ignore the federal government, thinking we're just faceless bureaucrats . . ."

Humphrey chortled. "We 'faceless bureaucrats' actually have all the power."

"Oh?" Wilkins laughed. "That's news to me."

"Everything we're taught about power within our government is wrong," Humphrey said, slurring his words slightly. "Presidents can get impeached. Members of Congress can lose their seats at any time. Or lose them in redistricting. There's the Supreme Court, I suppose, but they're mostly reacting to what the courts bring to them, and most of them have one foot in the grave already. Most of those we perceive as powerful are actually quite limited in their ability to use it, and lose it surprisingly easily. CEOs get tossed by their boards of directors all the time. The Wall Street titans lay awake at night fearing a sudden market crash. Hollywood stars live in fear that their next picture will flop. A professional athlete can be king of the city, and then suddenly one twist of your knee and it's all over. No, most of the people perceived as powerful have a quite tenuous hold on their stature."

Humphrey didn't need it, but he poured himself the dregs of one of the wine bottles and continued.

"But in the middle of the most power-conscious city in the hemisphere, plugging away, is the civil service. Presidents come and go, congresses come and go, and yet free from scrutiny and unmolested, tens of thousands go about their business, writing the rules, choosing what is and what is not really enforced, and spending millions upon millions."

Now Wilkins couldn't help giggling. "Kneel before the power of the deputy administrative director!" he bellowed in mock authority.

"Visible power, like demanding others kneel, is what makes you a target," Humphrey said with a shake of his head. "But power isn't always visible. People think we're paid poorly, but I am a GS-15, Step-8, whose salary is given the Washington locality adjustment of an additional 22 percent;[13] the benefits are

---

13 In 1983, Humphrey would be making about $87,000. In 2012 dollars, that would be roughly $195,000.

generous, with paid personal days, and near-total job security. Unused sick leave credit at retirement. Matched contribution to retirement benefits. Retirement health care. Quite a bit of domestic travel with per diems, and international, too. I make more than most of those in the private sector, with no fear of layoffs, and pay cuts are effectively impossible."

Wilkins sat and stared at his boss, strangely convinced—and in fact, strangely convincing—that he anonymously enjoyed a power-to-scrutiny ratio that would make the president green with envy.

"So you're saying that we're the ones who really rule Washington?"

Humphrey nodded.

"Okay, you are *drunk*. No way you're driving home tonight. I'm calling you a cab."

3

MARCH 1993
U.S. National Debt: $4.2 trillion
Budget, USDA Agency of Invasive Species: $72.6 million

M any new faces arrived in Washington in 1993, but five would prove most influential on the Agency of Invasive Species.

A trio of young women began work at the agency in the spring: communications office staffer Lisa Bloom, conference and event coordinator Jamie Caro, and technology systems analyst Ava Summers.

They had been hired around the same time by Carl, a crusty gray-haired veteran of the human resources department, who had moved to the Department of Agriculture from the Pentagon because he wanted something simpler and less bureaucratic. The three young women, all attractive, became derisively nicknamed "Carl's Angels" by agency veterans, cynical about attractive young women being hired by older men. Yet when a coworker called them that to their faces, the three laughed it off and instantly struck the gun-holding poses.

Lisa Bloom, a bright-eyed, freckled brunette, aspired to

emulate the new White House press secretary, Dee Dee Myers. Like most of the young women in Washington, Lisa had a not-so-secret crush on George Stephanopoulos. She once saw him at an Au Bon Pain in Foggy Bottom and squealed that he had been even more adorable in person, "like a little Chihuahua in an Armani suit."

She was quick to insist it was not mere lust that drove her Stephanopophilia but what he represented—that he was not much older than they were and yet he had already worked his way to the heights of power and influence. Only thirty-two, he already enjoyed a trusted relationship with the president of the United States. Lisa was certain that in this new era, a calcified, stodgy old order would be thrown off and that the world would finally see that a woman as young as herself could help set the agenda of the entire federal government.

As a political science major and College Democrat at the University of Maryland, Lisa had checked all the boxes of the young and politically minded, like protesting the Gulf War as another Vietnam and emphasizing the importance of a president familiar with the latest developments in supermarket checkout line technology. But what had most bugged her was how government itself had become this distant, out-of-touch entity. Under President George H. W. Bush, the federal government was a bunch of guys in wire-rimmed glasses whose sole purpose was to publicize drug war seizures and to complain about sitcom storylines. To *those* people, she would complain, the primary purpose of government was to hide embarrassment of the vice president.

Worst of all, Lisa thought, in 1992 America had endured unbelievable economic deprivation that had lasted for months—unemployment had reached 7.8 percent! She had been too young to vote in 1988 but proudly voted for Clinton in 1992, with *Rolling Stone*'s Jann Wenner promising, "he'll be the first rock and roll president in American history."[14]

With the end of the Cold War, government could finally serve the people the way it meant to, and that meant communicating more directly, more effectively, and more openly. Even about weeds.

The Agency of Invasive Species wasn't the most glamorous government public affairs job, but Lisa figured that she ought to have some government experience under her belt before she started working on campaigns. She had her career carefully planned out already: In 1996, she would become a press secretary on some Democrat's senatorial campaign, and by 2000, she would be Al Gore's press secretary, before becoming White House press secretary in January 2001.

She wished she could skip a step or two; she was more interested in articulating a policy than touting a particular candidate. A part of her feared that being a press secretary for a candidate would feel kind of dirty and degrading, like a year-long sales pitch.

Jamie Caro was a blond burst of sunshine within the gray corridors of the Department of Agriculture. While all of Carl's Angels cut strikingly attractive figures, the cheery Jamie endured the most relentless attention from men (and the occasional woman).

Jamie's father, a Miami lawyer, had the bejeezus scared out of him during the Cuban Missile Crisis and spent her childhood a bit obsessed about a peaceful end to the Cold War. While other South Florida families talked about the Dolphins or Hurricanes at the dinner table, Jamie's family discussions were heavily weighted toward the deployment of Peacekeeper

14 Joe Eszterhas, *American Rhapsody*, p.3.

missiles in Western Europe, the Strategic Defense Initiative, Soviet aggression in Afghanistan, the shooting down of KAL 007, and all other minute movements in the Doomsday Clock.

She grew up with her father glued to the television and radio during the big summits—Geneva, Reykjavik, Moscow, Washington. Her father was elated at the fall of the Berlin Wall, and at the University of Miami, Jamie studied international affairs. She relished the romance and grandeur of international diplomacy, and believed that history was made at summits like Malta.

She had thought about getting a master's degree and interning at the United Nations, but the AIS job gave her a chance for some quick experience in government, a steady income, health insurance, and, she hoped, a chance to make some connections in Washington. While she knew little about agriculture, she knew invasive species could be an international issue and figured she might, someday, organize some worldwide summit on locusts for the UN.

The third young woman creating a stir in the Department of Agriculture hallways was Ava Summers. She quickly became known as "Fishnets" for her stockings, fairly out of place within the staid federal workplace.

Early in her tenure, one short-lived boyfriend urged her to not wear them to work.

"You look like a hooker."

"I majored in computer science. I'm a girl who can quote *Star Trek*. I work for a federal agency that studies weeds. I did it with you up against a wall the night we met when everybody told me you were a standard-issue preppie. When do you think I started caring what other people think?" she asked.

And that was the end of that boyfriend.

Like many in Washington, Ava was smart, and also like many, restless and eager to leave a mark on the world. If you were young and wanted to make a lot of money, you majored in finance and set your sights on Wall Street. If you craved fame, you set out for Hollywood; rumor had it they were handing out sitcoms to stand-up comedians at LAX. If you wanted to invent some amazing new gadget or tool, you went to Redmond, Washington, or to Silicon Valley. But if you came to D.C., you were driven by something bigger.

The focus of that drive could be almost anything—abortion, foreign policy, the environment, economics. Young people in Washington tended to know a bit, or even a lot, about something beyond themselves and the pop culture of the moment. The twentysomethings of the nation's capital tended to be a little more interesting to talk to than their flannel-wearing peers elsewhere, who had dreams of fame and fortune but little sense of how to get them.

To the rest of the country, Washington was boring and stuffy; to the young people inside the Beltway, it was Nerdvana, an endangered-species preserve for geeks. It was a national dumping ground for all the folks who cared a lot about things that most people didn't care about much at all—the rights of women in Afghanistan, or the habitat of the snail darter, or aggressive Chinese naval maneuvers off Taiwan, or suburban sprawl, or early childhood foreign language education, or the homeless.

It wasn't merely the fishnets that made Ava stand out when she walked to work; she had a tongue ring, liked to add pink streaks to her straight black hair, and for all her reflexive dismissal of "girly" interests, her wardrobe seemed to be always changing. She grew bored easily, and her caffeine intake ensured that her mind tended to move in frenetic spasms of creativity.

Yet in between her effortless flirtation and voracious appetite for complicated ideas and topics that intimidated all but the übergeeks, she had a big vision: Ava believed that with the Cold War ending and this mysterious "Internet" coming down the pike, a few millennia's worth of top-down decision-making in human history was ending and an era of collective networks was coming. She foresaw a society unleashing previously unthinkable capacities of human potential, just around the corner. Soon gobs of information would flow in every direction, with less restriction and fewer gatekeepers. Eventually these quantum leaps in technology would leave everyone connected to one another, eradicating usual limits of distance and physical barriers.

It didn't take much to get her talking about these topics, and she often left listeners excited and confused.

As for why she was working at the agency, she believed that rapidly changing technology could usher in a new era of government being responsive to the needs of the public. Finally, government would *work*.

Of course, in her first days there, Ava thought she had stepped into a time machine, as all of the computers were from the late 1980s.

· · ·

The other two important arrivals of 1993 were President Bill Clinton and Vice President Al Gore.

It was March when Bill Clinton announced that his National Performance Review—more commonly known by its slogan, "Reinventing Government"—would be headed by Gore. A T-shirt sold on the street outside the White House featured Gore and Clinton as MTV's pair of losers, Vee-Pee-vus and Bubba-head, with the slogan, REINVENTING GOVERNMENT . . . 'CAUSE IT SUCKS!

It was not long before Humphrey again huddled with

Wilkins, having heard that Gore's task force was eyeing the Agency of Invasive Species as a fairly easy cut.

The timing could not have been worse, as Humphrey had lamented that the agency was operating under increasingly cramped quarters in the Department of Agriculture building, and was readying a proposal for a new, separate building. Now he would have to justify existing funding, never mind persuading others to spend money on a new state-of-the-art facility. Wilkins was less enthused about moving; the USDA building was a short walk from the Tidal Basin and he liked eating his lunch outside.

The pair sat on a bench, eating sandwiches on a spring day, as Humphrey contemplated his strategy for a new round of meetings with Gore and his advisers.

Wilkins greeted their latest challenge incredulously. "You can't tell me we survived twelve years of right-wingers, only to have the vice president try to ax us. How can this be happening again?" he asked. "I thought this was why we elected Democrats!"

"Don't stop thinking about tomorrow," Humphrey chuckled. "Gore was never a fan of ours in the Senate. Apparently his fellow tobacco farmers complained that we were slow to respond to their requests and insufficiently focused on the needs of Tennessee's agricultural community."

"Yeah, but cutting our budget? Would Hargis and the Appropriations Committee even allow that?"

"Jack, the president won the election with the lowest percentage of the popular vote in eighty years. To enact any significant portion of his agenda, he needs to dissuade the public of the notion that he is a big-spending liberal. He and Gore must find some areas to cut, and he will tout, with great fanfare, his list of cuts, even though they will be small."

"Why so small?"

"Because the president *is* a big-spending liberal. He will attempt to obscure a tax hike of thirty-five billion dollars[15] by cutting existing funding by about two billion.[16] Remember, much of the public is vague on the distinction between numbers ending in 'illion'; anything past seven figures is a synonym for 'a lot.' Diligence requires me to assume that our budget will represent a convenient and tempting target to reach their desired level of cuts."

Wilkins continued to moan. Humphrey ignored him and continued his lesson.

"Right now, Gore and his band are looking for scapegoats and sacrificial lambs, and this is a particularly unhealthy development for us. An unwatched budget tends to thrive, healthily—adjustments to the baseline and such. But the one thing that can get an agency's budget sliced to the bone is turning it into an UMA."

"Thurman?"

"An Unfortunate Memorable Anecdote. The six-hundred-dollar toilet seat. The five-hundred-dollar hammer. The joke that ends up in the monologue of Johnny Carson or that new fellow with the chin. If something big and embarrassing enough comes to light, and it creates days and weeks of headlines, it can become a symbol and Congress will make an example of it. Sure, you can always get the money back years later—it's not like they cut off Pentagon funding because of expensive toilet seats—but a federal agency's budget can be cut or frozen for years because of one sufficiently denounced and mocked mis-

---

15 Jerry Tempalski, "Revenue Effects of Major Tax Bills," OTA Working Paper 81, Office of Tax Analysis, US Treasury Department, July 2003.

16 *Common Sense Government Works Better & Costs Less*. Third report of the National Performance Review, September 1995, amount attributed to "changes in individual agencies."

take. You become so radioactive that no one on the Appropriations Committee can run the risk of funding you."

"Well, we'll just have to not have any waste, then," Wilkins chirped.

Humphrey shot him a disappointed look. "Jack Wilkins, any large organization has waste. There are simply too many variables, too many employees, too many decisions made in any organization to not have it. In fact, if you add various checks and balances and safeguards and precautions to avoid wasteful decisions, you end up with a slow and complicated system that spreads accountability so thin that it ultimately just adds to the waste. I've studied this for years, and there are only two solutions, neither of which fits our agency or many others."

"Try me," sighed Wilkins. "There's a tiny part of my soul that still believes in good government, and you seem eager to crush it."

Humphrey ignored the sarcasm and continued the lecture.

"The usual cry is to create financial incentives for efficiency, but even that comes with a cost. Here in the public sector, we are freed from the wolf at the door, referred to so euphemistically as 'creative destruction.' We don't focus on saving money; we focus on our jobs. You can't get things done if you're constantly chasing your tails looking for savings, driven by a nightmare of the whole place running out of money."

"Oh, we have that here, too. Even the U.S. government runs out of money at some point."

Humphrey laughed and dismissed the thought with a wave. "The second involves changing the culture of the organization, and while that is theoretically possible, I doubt we'll see it in our lifetime."

"What's wrong with our culture?" Wilkins asked.

Humphrey laughed. "Where to begin? For starters, how

many of our colleagues back in the office would you describe as having great drive and relentless professionalism? Some, no doubt. But a certain portion of those attracted to the public sector's work are looking for . . . a *different pace* than the one demanded elsewhere. A certain stability of eight-hour days leading to a secure retirement, with a certain . . . flexibility in quality control. You notice no one ever says, '*close enough for private sector work.*'"

Wilkins rolled his eyes. "You cynic."

"That tiny part of your soul that believes in a 'good government' ideal requires you to avert your eyes from the segment of the civil service that is attracted to the work precisely because it doesn't really want to work."

. . .

Al Gore met with reporters in a conference room in the Old Executive Office Building shortly before his meeting with the management of the Agency of Invasive Species. He showed the press an ashtray.[17] More precisely, it was a standard, regulation, federal government "ash receiver, tobacco, desk type," and Gore had ten pages of regulations to prove it.

He pointed to the federal specifications for testing the safety of the ashtray: Place the ashtray on a plank, and hit it with a steel punch "point ground to a 60 percent included angle" and a hammer. "The specimen should break into a small number of irregularly shaped pieces, no greater than 35."

Gore explained that stories of endless red tape undermined Americans' faith in government, and that he would spearhead an effort to eliminate waste, fraud, and abuse. Once he had restored Americans' faith in the competence and judgment of

17 Joe Klein, *The Natural*, pp. 64–65.

those who govern them, they would then embrace a muscular, activist role for government in areas like health care.

. . .

"Wait a minute . . ." Wilkins said, looking around the conference room within the Old Executive Office Building. "I've been in this room before."

Woodrow Wilson's portrait had replaced that of Calvin Coolidge, and Jack Kennedy had replaced Dwight Eisenhower. Wilkins and Humphrey were awaiting the arrival of the vice president and his team, a meeting that represented their last shot at removing themselves from the REGO chopping block.

With only a slight whirring of his mechanical joints and the hum of the powerful computer within his cranium almost entirely inaudible, Vice President Al Gore entered and activated "Reinventing Government Explanatory Monologue 46-C." He concluded:

"And that. My friends. Is why we. Are strongly considering. Reassigning the duties. Of this agency. To the Bureau of Agricultural. Resource Management. Rest assured. All efforts will be made. To minimize disruption. And you and your team. Will be given. Priority reassignment. In new roles. And duties. In other offices."

After an awkward silence, Humphrey began his defense. "Mr. Vice President, before you and your esteemed staff come to any final conclusions, I would like to read an assessment from a particularly wise voice on these matters."

Humphrey reached into his briefcase and removed a copy of *Earth in the Balance.*

"First edition, Mr. Vice President," Humphrey beamed. "With your permission, sir, I'd like to read aloud one passage that I found particularly relevant to this discussion."

Gore nodded, and the head-movement mechanisms within his neck were almost entirely inaudible.

"Page ninety-six: 'As the climate pattern begins to change, so too do the movements of the wind and rain, the floods and droughts, the grasslands and the deserts.'" He paused. "'*The insects and the weeds*, the feasts and famines, the seasons of peace and war.'"

One of Gore's aides couldn't stifle an awkward chuckle. Humphrey ignored him, and continued his eye contact with the vice president's optical sensors.

"Mr. Vice President, as you know, environmental research is drastically underfunded considering its importance not merely to the country but to the very survival of our species itself. The fine workers of the Environmental Protection Agency no doubt do their very best, but their attention to the particular threat of climate change–driven invasive species infestations is spotty, and I'm being kind. As a man of science, you understand how much vital work is dismissed and mocked by an ill-informed public. As a federal agency dealing with the threat to our agriculture, economy, and public health from weeds, you can imagine how many *Little Shop of Horrors* jokes we've endured over the years. We are perpetually ridiculed, ignored, derided, and dismissed as a waste. But you know better, sir. You know the importance of our mission, and how vital it will prove in the coming years of global warming. Unfortunately, I do not exaggerate when I say that if you will not stand up for us, no one will."

Humphrey and his staff had prepared their traditional evocative visual aids. Gore stared down at the maps before him, which were projecting green waves of thorny tropical vines snarling the upper Midwest and Mid-Atlantic. One caricature depicted vines coiling around the St. Louis arch, and helpfully pointed out that Missouri had eleven electoral votes in the upcoming presidential election.

"A changing climate is a weed's best friend, Mr. Vice President," Humphrey warned gravely. "That is the unpleasant, but unavoidable fact. You could call it an . . . *inconvenient truth.*"

Somewhere within the central processing unit of Gore's cerebral cortex, the phrase stuck.

. . .

When Gore's "Reinventing Government" report debuted, the Agency of Invasive Species was surprisingly unmentioned. And the following year's budget proposal from the president urged an additional $15 million in AIS funding.

. . .

The concept of a popular culture stuck on "repeat" had been the staple of cranky commentators for years, but for a short time in the early 1990s, Americans suddenly decided that the 1930s were cool again.

An exhaustion with a few years of slacker grunge gave way to an embrace of swank. At the same time that cigarette smoking became socially comparable to ritual murder, the nation—and the capital—suddenly embraced cigar bars. Double-breasted suits and fedoras returned; all at once, the movers and shakers looked like they were running with Al Capone.

Whiskey and martinis flowed. Pints of thick stout poured. Clubs and bars played neo-swing and lounge music. It was, for many Washingtonians, the split second they were cool.

The epicenter of this temporal inversion was Ozio, a club at 1835 K Street, touting itself as the city's "premier martini and cigar lounge" offering two pleasures that had not too long ago seemed so dated as to be socially backward.

"All this place needs is firearms," chuckled one off-duty ATF agent.

Modeled after the Paris Metro of the 1930s, Ozio was a subterranean, dimly lit, art nouveau temple of the era's forbidden, or at least naughtier, pleasures. Every young thing inside was experimenting with hard liquor or cigars, what one had scoffed as "the drug of the 1990s," or at least a genuinely socially daring habit for an "I didn't inhale" era. (Of particular note to Washingtonians employed in the public sector, hard liquor and tobacco caused no complications in obtaining or renewing a security clearance.) The descriptions of the cigars rivaled those of the most ambitious sommelier: *Heavy, with a hint of Portobello mushroom and an overtone of a decaf latte.*[18] *"Busy, yet never precocious." "A touch of irony in its Freudian allusions, but satisfying with a deep, nutty flavor that somehow distinctly evokes prerevolutionary Havana."*

One of Washington's tallest pundits-in-training encountered an attractive young lady smoking a cheroot and asked her, "Do you really like that thing?"

"I guess. Hmm . . . not really," she chuckled as she blew smoke in his face.

He coughed. "Why are you smoking it, then?"

She replied with a you-just-don't-get-it smirk and left him alone in the clouds.

Celebrating one year of working at the agency, Lisa, Jamie, and Ava drank away their sorrows with selections from the martini menu. They weren't really full of sorrow; they mostly felt irritation that life in Washington was nowhere near as exciting as the movies made it appear. Hollywood had suddenly

18 "On Top of Old Stogie," *The Washington Post*, February 16, 1996.

started celebrating political heroes in a plethora of comedies: *Bob Roberts, Dave, The Distinguished Gentleman*. Michael Douglas was supposedly making a romantic comedy about a young, crusading Democratic president. But real life was, alas, boring and full of tedious, frustrating setbacks.

"It's because we're entry level," Jamie asserted. "If we were a few more rungs higher on the ladder, we wouldn't be dealing with all this."

Lisa examined the cigar some guy had offered her. "I think every computer in the building is, like, three years out of date."

Ava lit her cigar up effortlessly. "Try four," she snipped. "Everybody might as well be using abacuses. Actually, that would be easier, because there wouldn't be any old infrastructure to work around." She puffed on the cigar a bit, and concluded the image of a cigar was more to her liking than the actual taste. "I'm not even sure where to start, because from what I've seen, by the time anyone responds to my recommendations of what kind of equipment we need, it's obsolete by the time the purchase is actually approved." She savored a long sip of her martini, a "Montreal Madam"—Absolut Kurant, Grand Marnier, and a splash of cranberry juice.

"Just a few more rungs on the GS ladder, we'll have more authority and be able to do things the way they were meant to be," Jamie insisted, motioning to their waiter for a second Stockholm 75.

"I . . . should be director of communications," Lisa said, feeling the first wave of giddiness and tipsiness from her Negroni. "My boss is a translucent yes-man to Humphrey."

Lisa found work at the agency particularly frustrating. A quintessential type-A personality, she had, through hard work and determination, always been able to get what she wanted before this. Within the agency's Department of Communications, she had quickly deluged her boss with perfectly proofread memos with ideas she deemed ingenious and irrefutably exciting. The first four generated increasingly terse rejections. The fifth generated a meeting with Humphrey.

"I'm in a communications office. I thought the point of this job was to communicate," she said, quietly pleased with the direct simplicity of her plea.

"Communication is a dangerous weapon, my dear, only to be unsheathed carefully and when needed," Humphrey said. "We want to ensure the world is watching on our best days and looking elsewhere the rest."

"I'm not gonna quit," Lisa said, extinguishing her cigar into one of the club's deep ashtrays. "I can persuade these old dogs. The world's changing. The Internet. These guys don't even realize how much they're hurting themselves. The whole reason Americans distrust government is because of a lack of communication, and if agencies just opened up and communicated better, Americans wouldn't be so reflexively right-wing and antigovernment."

They concluded, with a mix of hope and certainty, that everything would change when they were promoted and out of these low-level positions. And then they danced.

They had hoped that the guys in the club would join them, but most of the men were content to drink, smoke, and watch them dance instead.

NOVEMBER 1994
U.S. National Debt: $4.7 trillion
Budget, USDA Agency of Invasive Species: $91.2 million

As the evening progressed, Humphrey consumed a bit more scotch than he had planned. While he had proven that he could get more money for the agency in every fiscal year since 1977, he had always worked with an easily distractible Republican president and a pliable, helpful Democratic Congress, or at least a Democratic House. One way or another, he always overcame resistance to his perennial argument that *yes, everyone agrees controlling spending is very important, and there are many other places to study closely for cuts in next year's budget, but the activities of the Agency of Invasive Species really need more funding than last year, not less.* Always. Year in, year out.

But tonight's election returns were showcasing the unthinkable: Republicans were winning on a scale not seen in fifty years. That blasted lunatic Newt Gingrich was about to become Speaker of the House.

Even worse, a familiar name had cropped up in some of the coverage of the impending political tsunami. In the outer suburbs of Philadelphia, one of the Congress's most easily forgettable political weather vanes, three-term Democratic representative Bob Leere, found himself suddenly saddled with all of the failures of Congress under the Clinton administration: Hillarycare. Tax hikes. An invasion of Haiti. A surgeon general who wanted to teach masturbation in schools. A baseball season that ended without a World Series.

The Republicans had found a square-jawed, middle-aged man who had impeccable Reaganite credentials, experience in government and Washington policy fights, and about a decade's worth of business success to self-finance much of his campaign. He spoke with particularly convincing passion when he pledged to hold the line on runaway costs and to wipe out wasteful spending. In fact, he kept using this metaphor of menacing, relentless *weeds* overrunning the garden and choking out the needed growth of the American economy.

Nicholas Bader . . . had been elected to Congress.

Humphrey simply couldn't get his mind around it; it was one of those names that never belonged in the same sentence as "elected official," like Sonny Bono—except that in the clearest sign that the world had spun off its axis, Bono was being declared a winner in a California House race.

Congressman Nick the Knife. *Representative* Big Bad Bader.

It was late, Humphrey's wife had urged him to come to bed twice, but he couldn't stop clicking through the channels, waiting for the moment that the anchor would shout, "Live from New York, it's Saturday Night!" and reveal that it had all been an elaborate prank. But no reassurance came. At least Ted Kennedy had survived his challenge from that wealthy Ken doll who would probably now fade into obscurity.

Suddenly, the phone in Humphrey's home office rang.

"Hello?"

"Humphrey . . . it's *me*."

Bader. In the background, Humphrey could hear the noise of a raucous victory party.

"I suppose congratulations are in order, Mr. Congressman-elect."

"Thank you, Humphrey, even though I know you don't mean that. I wanted to call you as soon as it was official. . . . I had thought about mentioning it in my victory speech tonight, but I figured you wouldn't see it in Washington."

"Bethesda," Humphrey corrected.

"Wherever. In my original draft, I thanked you, because it was the thought of you that made me decide to run for office."

"I don't know what to say to that, Mr. Congressman-elect," Humphrey said, making no effort to hide his disgust. "I'm sure you have many happy supporters to thank—those corporations, those polluters, those misers so eager to see government workers tossed out in the cold."

Bader laughed. "Oh, Humphrey . . . I can't wait to see you again. With subpoena power."

"I imagine we'll be seeing a great deal of each other over the next two years," seethed Humphrey.

"Oh, yes, you can count on that. Do you remember that night at the Kennedy Center, when I told you that someday I was going to cut your budget down to a big goose egg?"

Humphrey stared at the phone as the giddy congressman was briefly overcome by a laughing fit.

"I'm coming for you, Humphrey."

The line went dead.

The Republican Revolution was on its way.

4

P anic.
    "The United States Capitol: it looks the way it did yesterday, but after last night, oh, boy, have things changed," declared the morning show anchor, unable to repress a tone of slight incredulity. "Good morning, America. I'm Charles Gibson, and that Capitol is a very different building this morning. It is in Republican hands. *Solidly* in Republican hands. Indeed, the House is Republican, the Senate is Republican, the majority of governorships, now Republican. The nation, right now, it would seem, is now Republican."

Humphrey called a midday Agency of Invasive Species staff meeting. For much of the morning, second and third cups of coffee were consumed, the morning papers were reviewed, radios and televisions remained on, stirring disbelieving groans every time Bob Dole was mentioned as the new Senate majority leader. Fifty-two Republicans had knocked off incumbent Democrats in the House at the morning hour, with a few races waiting to be decided. Eight more Republicans in the Senate. Eleven more new Republican governors. Alabama senator

Richard Shelby, a Democrat, announced that he would switch parties.

"I guess he has to follow his principles," Jamie shrugged.

"His principle is that he doesn't want to be in the minority!" hissed Lisa.

The younger staff was abuzz. Neither Jamie nor Lisa had voted yesterday—as District of Columbia residents, the only meaningful votes they cast came on the day of the Democratic primary—but they knew they had witnessed history, and the atmosphere of crisis was a welcome interruption to the boredom that had dominated their first two years on the job.

Wilkins found their excitement off-putting.

"I've got a friend, works in the administration, policy analyst," Wilkins mumbled as they filed into the conference room. "He's working on the next year's budget proposal for the State Department. I called him this morning. He said, he came into his office, looked at a pile of paperwork about foreign aid allocations sitting on his desk, and thought, 'Should I toss this in the trash? Should I go forward as if nothing changed? Is there even going to *be* any foreign aid?' My God, what do we do now?"[19]

Jamie couldn't help but laugh. "This is kind of how I expected the government to respond to an alien invasion."

"Have you ever seen that alien autopsy video? The thing on the table looks an awful lot like Newt Gingrich with no hair," Lisa scoffed.

"This is no time for panic," declared a grave, and slightly hungover, Humphrey from the doorway. "In two months, a horde of Republicans will take office, none of whom have any appreciation for the work of this agency, and at least one who is determined to see all of us thrown out into the cold. This is a time to report to battle stations."

19 Matthew Continetti, *The K Street Gang* (New York: Doubleday, 2006).

He settled in at the head of the conference table, and began handing out thick folders of information.

"We will need to research every potential avenue of leverage, every operation in every district with a new congressman, how many jobs, farms, and other Americans are influenced by our operations. We will need to research the past statements of all incoming congressmen who could be on the committees that could affect us—Agriculture, Appropriations, House Oversight and Government Reform, the works." He sighed. "And then there is the new Speaker."

A new hire asked, "Do we have any offices in Gingrich's district?"

"Suburban Atlanta," Wilkins answered. "We've got no real presence in the district, so we can't claim he'll cut jobs in his own community."

Humphrey glanced down at a memo. "Any word from our allies in the pesticide industry?"

"They say they have some ties to DeLay, who's supposed to be making a run for majority whip," Wilkins said. "Might be something there, but it's early and tenuous. Wouldn't want to stake all our futures on it."

Humphrey turned to Lisa.

"Miss Bloom, this morning I asked you to begin reviewing every public utterance that Newt Gingrich had ever said about the federal workforce and the workings of government. Have you found anything useful?

"Um . . ." she began, a little stunned that after feeling largely ignored for two years, the administrative director suddenly expected her to have an idea of how to save the whole ship from sinking within a few hours. "Gingrich's election night party was hosted by a local conservative talk show host named Sean Hannity. In his speech last night, Gingrich promised, "Every bill or committee report filed in Washington will be available instantly on computer."

"Great, I was dreading a long wait to read the bill calling for the elimination of our jobs," Wilkins quipped.

Undeterred, Lisa continued, "But in a speech a few days ago, he said, 'When you see a large government bureaucracy, is it an inevitable relic of the past that can't be changed, or is it an opportunity for an extraordinary transformation to provide better services?' "[20] She looked around the room. "The fact that he's raising the question suggests that to him it's not resolved."

The looks from most of the senior staff were skeptical, with smirks and scoffs. Wilkins had a slightly kinder tone to the younger staff than most of the agency's management, but even he came across as a bit condescending.

"Lisa, it's great that you put in this effort, but I think you're probably giving these guys too much credit," he said. "These guys don't see nuance. He's holding up this idea of a theoretical perfect reform, some 'extraordinary transformation' as a fig leaf to hide the fact that he's really intent on chopping away all of us 'relics of the past,' as he so kindly put it. To dissuade him, you would have to offer such an . . . 'extraordinary transformation to provide better services' that he'd be left with his head spinning . . ."

Humphrey suddenly jostled to life and began looking through the stack of folders and reports before him. Whatever he was looking for, it seemed to be at the bottom of the pile.

"What . . ." he began, almost absentmindedly, "was . . . that mumbo-jumbo from the trollop in the tech department?"

Lisa and Jamie exchanged a look, knowing he had to be referring to Ava.

---

20 Actually from a speech by Gingrich to House Republicans, December 5, 1994.

Finally, Humphrey found what he was looking for. A report marked:

WEED.GOV

A WEB ADDRESS PORTAL PAGE DATABASE
INTERCONNECTIVITY SYSTEM

DECEMBER 1994

U.S. National Debt: $4.8 trillion

Budget, USDA Agency of Invasive Species: $91.2 million

In two years, Ava had barely interacted with Humphrey. Once in a great while, the IT department would press-gang her into helping with senior staff's frantic calls for help with their computers. She had heard all of the apocryphal IT horror stories: *Your mouse is not a foot pedal. The pop-out disk drive is not a cup holder. "You keep telling me, 'press any key'—where's the 'any' key?"*

If the Central Intelligence Agency was anything like the Agency of Invasive Species, Ava feared, any foreign power would be able to crack into any database by typing in the password "PASSWORD" or "1234." Her innovative, groundbreaking technique of turning the computer off and turning the computer on again usually generated amazed stares that would have been fit for witnessing alchemy.

Of course, since she was cuter than the usual tech-gnomes scurrying up from the IT department, she noticed men tended to call with new problems again, shortly after her first visit.

Now she was in Humphrey's office, and he and Wilkins were peppering her with intense questions about her proposal for her "Web address portal page database interconnectivity system"—queries that revealed they barely understood what it did, how it worked, and why it would be useful.

"So you're saying that we could share all of this information through joint-access databases, but . . . why wouldn't we just pick up the phone and tell the person the same information?" Wilkins asked.

"You can still do that, but with this, it doesn't matter whether the person is at their desk or wherever—the information is there, 24/7, for anyone to access and use as they need it," she explained, wondering why he didn't seem to grasp this the first two times she discussed how agency employees would use the system. "And we're talking about massive amounts of information. Data. Weed counts, everything we put into our reports. Data you can put into spreadsheets and charts and all of that."

"But that's what fax machines are for."

She sighed. "No more paper jams. No toner replacements. No more PC LOAD LETTER messages."

"What you're suggesting would take money, no doubt," Humphrey said, making some sort of calculation in his head. "Our current budget, clearly, does not include room for the expenditures necessary to bring this to fruition."

"Oh, almost certainly, but I don't think it would be *that* expensive, and in the long run—"

"No, Ms. Summers, that's fine. The cost is . . . an issue we will bring up in February's meeting. In fact, I may need you to emphasize that to our congressional friends."

She nodded, then realized the enormity of the task she was being asked to perform.

"Part of me can't believe this!" she said. "I have been waiting two years to get anybody in this building to listen to this, and now all of a sudden you want me to present all of this to members of Congress."

"This . . . technobabble may be all that stands between

ourselves and budgetary oblivion, Miss Summers," said Humphrey. "So it had better be good."

Wilkins took a long look at Ava.

"When we have the meeting, ditch the fishnets," he ordered. "If Gingrich answers our invitation, you'll be meeting with the first Republican Speaker of the House in forty years."

"She'll be speaking to a room full of men," Humphrey corrected. "Keep the fishnets."

He hastily sketched out a map of the agency's offices within the Department of Agriculture building.

"I want Gingrich and anyone who comes with him to come the long way through the offices though the conference room, and everyone looking their best—diligent. Professional. If I see any pictures of President Clinton, Hillary Clinton, or Vice President Gore on anyone's desk, I will set them on fire."

Ava was fairly certain Humphrey meant the desk pictures and not the occupants, but decided not to ask for a clarification.

"We need to ensure that the phones are ringing as they walk through—we want to greet them but also look busy, a beehive of activity. In the conference room, find some of the softer lightbulbs and find whatever old maps we have and frame them and mount them. Older the better, Civil War or Revolutionary would be ideal. I want the Speaker to wonder if he's wandered into the Smithsonian."

They exited Humphrey's office, looked at the bull pen of cubicles, and examined the conference room. Humphrey paced the path the visiting members of Congress would walk on the way to their meeting.

"And Wilkins, I don't care if you have to go scuba diving in the La Brea Tar Pits, we absolutely must have a mounted dinosaur bone!"

JANUARY 1995
U.S. National Debt: $4.815 trillion
Budget, USDA Agency of Invasive Species: $112.2 million

It was like a parade: The new congressmen kept coming—red ties, striped ties, comb-overs, white hair, no hair, pale suits, dark suits, striped suits, brown suits, the occasional woman in a red power suit. Mixed in with the crowds of the first day were the Mighty Morphin Power Rangers, who performed in the Longworth House Office Building cafeteria for the members and their families. Speaker Gingrich saluted the Rangers, declaring that they were "multiethnic role models" with an emphasis on "family values" and "anti-drug" messages that fit nicely with GOP political themes.[21]

Adam Humphrey did not want to leave any detail overlooked in the upcoming battle over the fate of the Agency of Invasive Species, and so he had been desperately trying to arrange every possible meeting with every remaining ally on Capitol Hill.

The second day of the new Congress, Humphrey had an emergency meeting with Congressman Hargis, who was distinctly cranky at being in the minority for the first time in his thirty-two years in office. On Humphrey's way out he was surprised to find Bader, who had apparently been lingering in the hallway, waiting for him.

"Hiya, Humphrey," Bader grinned.

"Mi—Congressman Bader," Humphrey gathered his composure. "Please tell me you've spent the entire day waiting in the hallway stalking me."

"My new office is just down the hall," Bader said with a

---

21 John M. Broder and Sam Fulwood III, "Gingrich's Gavel Sends a Signal to New Political Power Rangers," *Los Angeles Times*, January 5, 1995.

gleeful nod. "I had an intern watch Hargis's Temple of Pork and let me know when you entered."

"I'm sure the young lady is already finding her time in congressional service well spent."

"Well, we're a busy group, much to cut. The whole federal government's going to look a lot smaller pretty soon."

"I assure you, I've heard that pledge many times from your predecessors, Congressman."

Bader stepped a little too close for comfort. "Yeah, but we're not like the Republicans you've seen before, Humph," Bader said softly but with distinct menace. "We actually mean what we say."

"Mmm, yes, I was positively inspired when I saw the new majority leader declaring that perhaps term limits might no longer be necessary now that Republicans were running the show."[22]

Bader was enjoying his opportunity to gloat. "This is a revolution, Humphrey. We're gonna turn this town upside down. Your free ride just came to an end. This time it's different. We have public opinion on our side."

Humphrey's mood darkened, and his tone shifted slightly, as though he quickly tired of sparring with Bader.

"You have the shallow, superficial support of a voting public that has the attention span of an over-caffeinated ferret," Humphrey warned quietly. "We have jobs, pensions, benefits packages, careers, long-term contracts on the line. You are fighting for an abstract idea, while my allies and I are fighting for quite tangible benefits. Good luck, Congressman Bader. When the ground falls out beneath your feet, I will be there, smiling, reminding you that I warned you of this."

He turned away.

---

22 Bob Novak's foreword to Sen. Tom Coburn's book *Breach of Trust* (Nashville: Thomas Nelson, 2003).

"Better freshen up that resume, Humphrey!" Bader cracked as his old foe stormed away.

FEBRUARY 1995
U.S. National Debt: $4.854 trillion
Budget, USDA Agency of Invasive Species: $112.2 million

On his way into the Agency of Invasive Species' conference room, the new Speaker noticed that the *Time* magazine declaring him "Man of the Year" was front and center upon tables in both the lobby *and* a small table outside the conference room, and smiled.[23]

Newt Gingrich was a busy man, and some on his staff had doubted whether a meeting with agency officials was worth the time commitment. But one of the GOP's most intense freshman, a rising star from suburban Philadelphia, had been urging the new Speaker relentlessly that the agency should be among the first cuts enacted by the new GOP Congress. Gingrich found Bader a bit grating in his insistence, but when he heard that the agency's management had been desperately requesting a meeting with the new Speaker, Gingrich figured it was worth rolling his motorcade down Independence Avenue. Security, motorcades, a surrounding staff—Gingrich moved a lot like a president now, and he liked it.

He and his phalanx of dark-suited aides entered the conference room, where Humphrey, Wilkins, and assorted other

---

23 "The White House figured out how to play Newt," said Tony Rush, Tom DeLay's chief of staff. "They would put the *Time* magazine cover with Newt as the 'Man of the Year' on the coffee table in front of where they would have Newt sit. Newt would come back from leadership meetings with the White House and tell us how the White House understood his significance. And people would look around and say to themselves, 'Have you lost your mind?'" Steven M. Gillon, *The Pact: Bill Clinton, Newt Gingrich, and the Rivalry That Defined a Generation*, p. 153.

agency staffers awaited them, looking their best and trying to hide the sweat on their hands. Ava stood out like a pinup girl at an accountants' convention.

Wilkins had failed to secure a dinosaur bone as Humphrey had demanded—it turned out they were expensive and rare—and so they had found a mounted skull of a hippopotamus for sale from a university's biology department. They removed the small brass plaque identifying the species and hoped no one noticed. Once everyone was seated, it became clear that the giant skull would obstruct views across the table, and so Wilkins and another staffer moved it to the side table.

"I hope you appreciate the significance of my taking time to come here and illuminate your new role," Gingrich said as he settled in. "Very few people understand the scale of change that this past election brought, and how far-reaching it will be. Frankly, it takes a fundamentally, profoundly transformational figure like myself to implement a change on this scale. These figures have come along periodically in American history when the national spirit required it most: Washington at Valley Forge, Andrew Jackson at the Battle of New Orleans, Lincoln from Fort Sumter to the Battle of Five Forks . . ."

Judging from his waistline, he's been losing the battle of five forks, thought Wilkins.

"Theodore Roosevelt at San Juan Hill, Franklin Roosevelt after Pearl Harbor, and Ronald Reagan . . ." he paused, contemplating the right historical moment to cite. "Throughout his presidency," he concluded.

"The task before me involves harnessing my leadership in all of the manners they demonstrated, simultaneously—oh, and Edison and Woodrow Wilson, too—and enacting an unprecedented agenda of fundamental reform. We are an idea-oriented national campaign without a presidential leader yet, equaled only by Henry Clay and the War Hawks of 1810 and the Progressive movement of 1910."

Gingrich continued discussing the centennial echoes of his movement for ten minutes straight before a brief throat-clearing from an aide reminded him that he was supposed to be breaking the bad news to the collected agency employees.

"We are at a crossroads as a nation," Gingrich said. "We are fundamentally reevaluating the role between the citizen and government, and shifting the power away from unelected, know-it-all, smug, out-of-touch, Washington elitist bureaucrats." Gingrich looked around the room. "No offense."

"None taken, Mr. Speaker," Humphrey lied.

"We're shifting power toward the people, who indeed know what is best for themselves. It makes no sense to allocate millions upon millions to a federal agency just to keep track of what weeds and bugs are where and recommend what ways to treat it and allocate grants to farmers to ensure response. Not when every state has its own state-level agriculture department office doing the same, and many localities and agribusiness giants have their own research and efforts on these matters. It's enormously duplicative and redundant and, frankly, stupid. So at this point, we're preparing legislation to zero out the funding for this agency and convert it all to block grants, so that states can manage their own weed-abatement programs."

For a moment, Wilkins wondered if an ulcer could spontaneously form within a matter of seconds, as his stomach twisted and burned with new anxiety. *As bad as we feared*, he thought.

Humphrey gently drummed his fingers on the conference room table. "Mr. Speaker, while I disagree with the specific direction of your proposal, I must say your vision is positively Churchillian. Actually, I couldn't decide whether it was Churchillian or more like Charlemagne."

"I had debated that myself," Gingrich nodded. "In fact, I had actually seen echoes of Confederate Army Captain John Carter, who during the Barsoom campaign—"

"Mr. Speaker, I hate to interrupt," Humphrey said as he seized the floor, lest Gingrich be overcome by his urge to resume his history lecture. "But if you will permit me a moment to update you on our latest efforts to deal with the problems you have so rightly identified, I think we may have some ideas that are . . . appropriate to these historical national crossroads you so astutely foresaw. Our agency is going through a metamorphosis, Mr. Speaker, and at the heart of that all-encompassing change is *innovation*," Humphrey confidently declared, having memorized all of the futurist catchphrases from Gingrich's earlier books. "We believe that the clearest path to the freer, more prosperous future you envision is through 'Weed.gov,' a cross-referenced interactive database that exchanges information at the speed of electrons about how best to protect the American bounty from invasive species. Miss Summers?"

The fishnet-clad wonder popped out of her chair, checking to make sure her computer wires were all connected. She began showcasing a display that was like a slide projector, but used some software she had bought herself and brought into the building in violation at least six or seven different federal acquisition regulations. The mysterious "PowerPoint 4.0" icon disappeared and she began showcasing stock photography of people screaming and expressing frustration.

"Okay, the reason you and everybody on the Hill and everybody outside these walls is so batsh—er, bonkers with frustration at this agency, and all of them like this one, is speed—it takes forever for anything to get done. Somebody finds a weed in their crops, they want it dealt with, like, immediately. They want answers immediately. It's out there, and you know that *somebody* knows what it is and how to deal with it, and yet there are all these barriers. They have to take a guess on the best way to deal with it all, while they wait for their problem to work its way up the ladder, and wait for the answer to work its way down the ladder. By the time the answer reaches them, their problem may have completely changed."

She paused on an image of many arrows heading up a ladder, and many arrows heading down a ladder. The graphic carried the message:

LAYERS = RESPONSE TIME = WEED GROWTH = BAD

"Precisely!" Gingrich boomed. "That's it exactly. How old are you, nineteen?"

"Twenty-four," Ava answered.

"If she can understand this, why can't you old guys get this?" Gingrich asked with a smirk. He was kidding, but Ava's heart pounded a bit. At last, recognition! The Speaker of the House was in her office building, dressing down her bosses for not listening to her.

She switched to an image of a spiderweb, where all of the layers were connected with each other in concentric circles.

"What if you could connect everybody who ever worries about these things together so that information passes among them almost instantaneously? Instead of a farmer in Georgia and a state agricultural official in Florida and a pesticide manufacturer in Tennessee and someone here in Washington all responding to this separately and in periodic, static communication, what if they were all simultaneously coordinated? What if instead of this slow-moving, disconnected response, everyone in the system moved like a school of fish or flock of birds, separately but unified, to nip the problem in the bud? Our idea, Weed.gov, can do this."

Humphrey quietly cleared his throat.

"If you give us the funding to implement Weed.gov, we can

do this," she said, remembering Humphrey's emphatic instructions about phrasing. "This would be the collective hive mind of everyone in the entire country involved in growing anything, from the biggest agribusiness giants to small farmers to gardeners. Somebody spots an outbreak of Dutch Elm disease and BOOM! They post it and it gets catalogued. Our experts examine the particular threat to regional agriculture, the most effective responses, the most likely dispersal patterns. Information gets out to everyone who needs it, instantly. For once, information can actually outrun the invasive species themselves."

Newt stared in awe and glee.

"This is the most profound understanding of my revolutionary vision I have ever encountered from any federal government employee ever!" he said, practically bouncing out of his chair with enthusiasm. He looked at her in amazed delight. "I can't believe somebody finally gets it!"

This somehow turned Ava's enthusiasm up another notch. "Picture it: An online encyclopedia of all invasive and noxious weeds—tens of thousands of different species, categorized and cross-referenced. A photo-matching database so that any citizen could upload a photo of a particular weed and have an AI algorithm identify it."

Humphrey jotted down a note to himself: MAKE SURE AI DOES NOT DISPLACE HUMAN AGENCY EMPLOYEES.

"Think about how quickly we would know when some invasive species is in an area!" Ava continued. "Think about how comprehensive our responses would be. In the long run, this could save millions! Within a few years, this could make us so efficient that we could be twice as effective for half the cost. With this up and running, you could probably cut our budget with no drop-off in agency performance!"

Humphrey failed to entirely stifle a spit-take.

"Thank you, Miss Summers, this has all been very helpful, but we ought to remind the Speaker of the caution necessary for long-term budgetary assessments!" He wiped the mess. "So as you can see, Mr. Speaker, the block grant proposal favored by some in the House, such as Congressman Bader, might result in some short-term savings, but would ultimately result in a disjointed system of responses that proved even more redundant and slow moving because of communication issues between separate state agricultural offices. Contrast that with the innovative, effective, and truly groundbreaking approach of Weed.gov, well . . ."

"The digital revolution ending the era of bureaucracy and ushering in an era of ad-hoc-racy, a fluid, organically structured organization that adapts to changing challenges and circumstances," Gingrich beamed. "I'm very impressed, and considering that you're all just a bunch of government employees, I'm even more impressed."

"Don't be too impressed!" Ava exclaimed before Humphrey could steer away from the Speaker's lapse into condescension. "We've been trying to use the interagency working group as often as possible! It's just like Toffler wrote—"

"You *read* Toffler?!" exclaimed Gingrich in giddy disbelief.

"Hell-*lo*?" Ava laughed. "He's only the world's most famous futurologist, the foremost scholar on how technology advances change society, and the preeminent theoretician of the singularity!"

Humphrey had urged all of his senior staff to read up on Gingrich, but he hadn't told Summers to do this. He realized her enthusiasm was genuine.

For fifteen straight minutes, the Speaker of the House and Ava mind-melded on all manner of obscure scientific, technological, and sociological topics: Nanotechnology. Genetic engineering. Satellite-based handheld communications. Space exploration. They quickly mapped out a plan to build a *Star Trek*–level utopian society within a decade and a half.

"I keep telling people, the science that Michael Crichton based *Jurassic Park* upon is extremely doable, and would really not be that expensive, difficult, risky, or time-consuming!" said Gingrich with an incredulous irritation that seemed incomprehensible to everyone else in the room but Ava.

"Not when you can adjust the growth rate of the species by tinkering with its genetic code!" Ava said. "And who's to say you have to stop with dinosaurs? How much does the endangered species list change when we can whip up as many animals as we need in a lab to replenish the species? We could have flocks of dodos whenever and wherever we want! What happens when extinction becomes not just reversible, but obsolete?"

Wilkins leaned over to Humphrey. "This is going a little too well," he whispered. "It's getting creepy."

. . .

Gingrich stayed a half hour longer than scheduled, and talked with Ava all the way through the building to the front door. He hadn't explicitly promised funding to create Weed.gov, but his body language and tone suggested a transformative excitement.

Then . . . nothing happened. Weeks went by. Then months. No bad news came from the Hill—enacting the Contract with America was proving a time-consuming challenge for the new Republican majority—but no good news, either.

Until Humphrey's secretary received a call, inviting the administrative director to a meeting . . . with Congressman Bader. The new congressman already established himself as the rookie hell-raiser of the House Oversight and Government Reform Committee.

Humphrey and Wilkins reported to Bader's office, only to be

informed by the secretary that the congressman was expecting them . . . on the Speaker's balcony.

They reported to the Speaker's office, and Bader's head emerged from a doorway.

"This way, Humphrey. Leave your Boy Wonder," Bader cracked.

Wilkins glowered and left.

. . .

They emerged to a luxurious balcony, and past the wrought-iron gate was one of the most spectacular, and coveted, views in Washington. Just past a lawn lay the Ulysses S. Grant Memorial, beyond that a reflecting pool, a long expanse of the National Mall with the boxy Smithsonian museums on either side, and the obelisk of the Washington Monument. A noisy airplane made its ascent from National Airport. The sun was beginning to set. The traffic noise seemed distant. It was an oasis of relative quiet and open space compared to the cramped offices in the building behind them. Humphrey realized if he had a balcony like this, he might never step back inside his office.

Bader lit up a cigar, and offered one to Humphrey.

"John Hay," he said, not removing it from his mouth. "Named after Lincoln's secretary. They grow the tobacco in my district."

"No thank you, Congressman, my preferred vice is any brown liquor in fine crystal." The two men stared out at the mall for a moment, and then Humphrey felt compelled to break the silence. "This is a most kind and . . . suspicious invitation. I figured that to ever enjoy this view, I would need an invitation from the Speaker himself."

"Newt allows me to use it." Bader buffed and looked Humphrey up and over. "He and I are getting pretty chummy lately."

Humphrey sensed there was a bitterness beneath the bragging, and his mind began calculating, analyzing, out loud, almost uncontrollably. "He has given you a special privilege. . . . He did this because he needed something from you . . . or if he needed to placate you. By any chance, has the Speaker decided to abandon the effort to cast my staff and me to the fiery pits of budgetary oblivion?"

Bader nodded, and continued to stare out toward the horizon. "Newt says he's . . . putting my bill to eliminate the agency on the back burner. Wrong fight at the wrong time, he says."

Humphrey managed to stifle any laughter, but not the smile. "I had been hearing something along those lines."

"And he seems to be gung-ho about this magic computer system you sold him on," Bader growled.

"Weed.gov," Humphrey declared.

"Right," Bader said, although his tone made clear he couldn't possibly care less about the name of the system. "So . . . in the interest of . . . cooperation between your agency and my colleagues, I was willing to go along with the funding for this weed-picker-dot-com thing if you could point to some other program that you deemed . . . expendable."

Ah-ha, thought Humphrey. *He can't cut all of my budget, so he wants to find a piece to save face.* "Within the agency or elsewhere within the federal budget? Because I've always found congressional fact-finding missions to exotic overseas destinations to be a particularly unnecessary portion of our governing expenditures. Bringing the spouses along seems like an unnecessary expense as well—"

"Within your agency," Bader said, shooting Humphrey a glare that could, by itself, trigger a hostile-workplace complaint. "Surely, any good administrative director could think of some expenditures of his agency that can be eliminated or cut back so that funds can be reallocated to a new computer system."

Humphrey drummed his fingers on the railing.

"Unfortunately, Congressman, nothing is coming to mind off the top of my head. I would need to look at our most recent budget figures," he said, shaking his head. He backed away, sensing that the meeting's purpose was clear and there was no point in hanging around.

"Take a look," Bader said. "After I get some specific and substantive suggestions and figures, I would . . . really enjoy having you back up here, to . . . enjoy some brown liquor in fine crystal."

"Your hospitality is most kind, Congressman," Humphrey lied. "And I'll get on that as soon as possible. My study of Washington has taught me to always partake of an invitation from a congressman when given the chance," he smiled as he prepared to twist the knife. "Because you never know how long they'll be in a position to offer that invitation."

Bader's mouth smiled, but his eyes didn't.

HEARING TESTIMONY
HOUSE OVERSIGHT AND GOVERNMENT REFORM COMMITTEE
HEARING ON MANAGEMENT PRACTICES OF THE U.S. DEPARTMENT OF AGRICULTURE & ASSOCIATED PROGRAMS
JUNE 5, 1995

Chairman: The gentleman's time has expired. And the next round of questioning, five minutes time allocated, goes to my distinguished colleague from the great state of Pennsylvania, Mr. Bader.

Rep. Nicholas Bader, R-Pa.: Thank you, Mr. Chairman. I'd like to direct my questions to Mr. Humphrey. Administrative Director Humphrey, how many employees does the USDA Agency of Invasive Species have?

Humphrey: I'm sorry, Congressman, could you repeat the question?

Bader: I said, how many federal government employees work at your agency?

Humphrey: Well, that is a different question than your first inquiry, Congressman.

Bader: I'm sorry, what?

Humphrey: Apology accepted, Congressman, but the categories of "employees" and "federal government employees" are not necessarily synonymous. We have contract workers and seasonal workers and unpaid interns and others who do not fit the accepted definition of "federal government employees." So you are asking for two different figures here.

Bader: Okay, fine. Give me both figures.

Humphrey: Ah. Congressman, because we are on the record and lying to Congress is a crime, I am afraid I must be circumspect in my assessments of these figures. I would much rather leave a question unanswered than provide inaccurate information to Congress.

Bader: It's a head count, Mr. Humphrey, not calculus. Give me a figure.

Humphrey: Congressman, the precise figure is constantly changing with new hires and retirements; it's unclear if your request includes part-time workers, contract workers, and those on maternity, sick, and other leave; it is unclear how to count those whose primary duties are in interagency working groups, it is unclear whether to count unpaid interns and paid interns; it is unclear whether to count those who contribute to agency publications. Also, because of the seasonal nature of agricultural work, the workload of our agency and the personnel required tend to change with the seasons as well.

Bader: I just want a number.

Humphrey: Well, I can give you a number, but I believe you would prefer a number that comes closest to representing the constantly changing actual figure. Perhaps this matter could be most easily resolved if I gave you a range.

Bader: Fine. Give me a range.

Humphrey: Shall I begin with the floor of the possible range of employees of the agency as of this moment, or the ceiling?

Bader: The floor, Mr. Humphrey.

Humphrey: Very well.

(Humphrey consulted with counsel at this point.)

Humphrey: Congressman, our agency counsel recommends that I provide the floor figure of "one hundred."

Bader: One hundred employees? That doesn't seem a little low to you?

Humphrey: Congressman, I share your frustration, and would inform you that I dissuaded our counsel from his original suggested floor figure of zero.

(laughter)

Chairman: The committee will come to order.

Bader: Mr. Humphrey, I'm going to keep my language civil for the moment and declare that that number is not particularly illuminating. What's your ceiling?

(Humphrey consulted with an aide at this point. The consultation continued for several moments.)

Bader: Mr. Chairman, how long until I can hold the witness in contempt of Congress?

Chairman: Simmer down, Mr. Bader. Mr. Humphrey?

Humphrey: Mr. Chairman, I can inform you that the agency has a ceiling of two hundred thousand employees.

Bader: Really? Not a million? You guys feel safe ruling out the possibility that you have a million employees right now?

Humphrey: We do, Congressman.

Bader: Because there are currently about 175,000 Marines in the U.S. Armed Forces, and I think it says everything we need to know about the federal government that it's even remotely possible that we have more federal workers picking weeds than serving in the Marine Corps. Furthermore, I have the testimony of the Secretary of Agriculture right here, who puts the number of employees of his entire department at around one hundred thousand.

Humphrey: As I thought I made clear, Congressman, the figures at issue are only a rough estimate of a constantly changing figure that—

Bader: Mr. Humphrey, what I think you're doing is obfuscation designed to keep this committee and the public in the dark about just how large your agency has grown in the twenty years since its founding, and obscuring just what the American people get for the millions upon millions they have poured into your agency over the years. This kind of—

Chairman: The gentleman's time has expired.

NOVEMBER 1995
U.S. National Debt: $4.98 trillion
Budget, USDA Agency of Invasive Species: $112.2 million

The reports of a breakdown in budget talks had been growing louder, but no one had believed that differences between the new Speaker and President Clinton would lead to an actual shutdown of the United States government. Wilkins had periodically reassured the workers beneath him, "We're the federal government. We never close."

But as the deadline approached, the unbelievable had become reality. Congress had failed to appropriate any money to pay the salaries after the next pay period. The Agriculture

Secretary had given the word: Be ready to operate only with essential personnel starting the day after tomorrow.

Humphrey gathered all of his employees in a crowded conference room. Some stood in the hallways; those in field offices listened by conference call.

"Women and children first," Humphrey declared.

"You had to evoke the *Titanic* right off the bat, huh?" Wilkins groaned.

"I approach the decision of 'vital personnel' with some chivalry," Humphrey explained. "I am certain, once the shutdown ends, we will all be reimbursed for missed pay periods. Higher-salaried staffers are more likely to have accumulated savings to use for expenses during this time than our newer and younger workers. So, despite the fact that my instructions indicate that the younger among you are likely to rank among the nonessential, I . . . interpret the definitions differently than the Office of Management and Budget guidelines suggest. Any of you who find yourself with dire financial expenses in the near future, send me a memo by the end of the day and I will see to it you are deemed 'essential.' Those of you who can afford a delayed paycheck or two, your temporary sacrifice is appreciated. Beyond these arrangements, I myself will be . . . able to make emergency loans to anyone who needs it."

Wilkins looked around the room and saw expressions of surprise and awe. For all of his flaws, Adam Humphrey believed in protecting his people.

"How long will the shutdown last?" Jamie asked.

"That's up to the president and Congress, but I am taking steps to assure that we are in the innermost of inner loops as this fiscal crisis is resolved," Humphrey said with a strangely reassuring, confident tone. "For some of you, this will be a brief unexpected vacation."

A mix of disbelief, nervous laughter, and gallows humor as the workers paraded out. A shell-shocked Wilkins was left alone in the room with Humphrey.

"So how are we getting into the innermost of inner loops?" he asked.

"You and I are about to become surgically attached to Congressman Hargis."

SUNDAY, NOVEMBER 19, 1995

It was the first time Wilkins had been back to the White House since he worked there under Carter.

"I . . . am thrilled to be back here, Congressman, but shouldn't you be back at the Hill?"

"I'm here to tell them we are up a creek," Hargis grumbled as he, Humphrey, and Wilkins sat, shoulder-to-shoulder and butt-cheek-to-butt-cheek on a couch in the West Wing hallway.

"Forty-eight of my Democratic colleagues just voted for the Republicans' continuing resolution that would require the president to submit a proposal to balance the budget within seven years. To do that, we would have to *cut*—not reduce the rate of growth, *cut*—about $160 billion from what we're spending now."

"Absolute madness," Humphrey said, shaking his head. "Just keeping our budget static, with no baseline adjustments in the coming seven years, would be unthinkable. . . . To meet that insane ideological goal, every government agency would have to cut spending . . . one and a half percent in seven years!"

"More, really, because they would have to exclude entitlements," Wilkins murmured.

Hargis ran his fingers through his thinning silver hair. "I'm getting hell in my district, and that never happens. I have to look like I want to balance the budget. And if somebody like me is flipping, there's no way we can sustain a veto from Clinton."

Humphrey was as pale as Wilkins had ever seen him.

"My God . . . it's going to happen, isn't it? These barbarians are actually going to . . ."

"Lucky me," Hargis chuckled bitterly. "I get to be the one to tell Bill Clinton that for the first time since World War II, the federal government will spend less than the year before."

Through a window, they caught a glimpse of Clinton in his sweatsuit, reentering the Oval Office. A young brunette aide—an unpaid intern, most likely—emerged from the doorway and told the congressman the president would be ready to see him in a moment.

Hargis entered, and Humphrey and Wilkins were left on the couch, thankfully able to put some space between them. They sighed and looked at each other.

Wilkins was groping for a way to say things wouldn't be that bad when they suddenly heard an explosion of howling laughter and cheers from a few offices away.

"YEE-HA!"

Several people roaring, laughing, and cheering. Coming from the direction of the Oval Office, Wilkins thought. They rose, walked toward the door, hesitated to open it, and then paced.

After several minutes, Hargis burst out, exuberant and laughing.

"We dodged a bullet!" The overweight congressman was somehow jumping up and down, and he slapped the men on their shoulders like an offensive lineman who recovered a fumble to score a touchdown. Beyond the doorway, they could hear the giddy cheers continuing. "Those sons-of-bitches just faxed over a continuing resolution proposal that makes the concessions we wanted on Medicaid, Medicare, education, and the environment. All they wanted in return was some window dressing on veterans and defense spending."

"The Republicans?" Wilkins asked.

"Blinked!" concluded Humphrey.

"Does this mean we won't get cut?" Wilkins asked.

"It means the shutdown's over, at least until mid-December," Hargis said. He had to sit down after his little touchdown dance of celebration. "Hoo . . . We're not out of the woods yet, but at least now we've got a shot. Those fools just declared a temporary ceasefire before we could hand them our surrender papers."

"A proposal like this means that someone over there is sweating," Humphrey surmised. "If they concede this now, they'll probably be likely to concede something else, later."

DECEMBER 1995

The shutdown ended . . . and then it began again.

The offices had reopened, and then, like déjà vu, the closure repeated. Once again, most federal workers remained home—as the holidays were approaching, some didn't mind—and the news was full of breathless reports of the latest tense negotiations.

Humphrey once again began shadowing Hargis, ostensibly to keep the congressman informed about how the shutdown affected agency operations. But Wilkins knew that for the first time, Humphrey felt genuinely powerless about his work, and his "advice" to Hargis was becoming less veiled and subtle with every conversation. Wilkins sensed that if you took Humphrey's work away from him, he might lose his mind.

Humphrey and Wilkins were supposed to meet the congressman on Capitol Hill. Hargis wasn't leading the negotiations but remained on their periphery. As an appropriator, his duty was periodically to remind the White House that they could not make concessions about spending, which his Democratic colleagues in the House considered their divine right. The White House was also counting on Hargis to win over Republicans who had been on the Appropriations Committee for a long time, nudging them to get them to urge their hardline colleagues to concede. Thankfully, Hargis and his fellow Democrats had allies on the Appropriations Committee staff, almost all of whom were holdovers from when the Democrats were running the committee a year earlier.

So a few days before Christmas, Wilkins and Humphrey found themselves wandering the halls of the Senate office buildings, with Humphrey beginning to wonder if Hargis was deliberately avoiding him.

"Are they meeting in Dole's office, or in Daschle's office?" Wilkins asked.

Humphrey opened a door on the other side of the room, and entered one of the nicer meeting rooms he had ever seen on Capitol Hill. The room had a fireplace, and was fragrant with pine. Outside, a few flurries could be seen outside the window, which was flanked by long, gold curtains. A plate of cookies sat on the table.

"Oooh, cookies!" Wilkins's face lit up. He crossed the room, reached for one—and then heard one of the doors on the other side of the room being unlocked.

Wilkins shot a panicked look at Humphrey, and ducked behind the gold curtain. Humphrey glared but followed, and the pair stood silently as they heard two familiar voices enter.

"In here, George—this back room," said a flat, low Kansas twang. "The fireplace keeps it warmer—I'm starting to wonder if you guys got the building folks to turn down the heat, trying to freeze us out."

"Wouldn't dream of it, Senator," replied the young, cheerily chirping George Stephanopoulos with a laugh.

"Moravian spice cookie?"

"Thank you, Senator," Stephanopoulos replied. "Not where we were supposed to be right before Christmas, huh? An incumbent president, a likely challenger, stuck in Washington, far from the primary states."

"Ergh. Argh. I've got to get to New Hampshire," Dole muttered, tugging on his cardigan sweater with his left hand. "One way or the other, this thing is over on the thirty-first, because I'm out of here."

Stephanopoulos nearly choked on his cookie, and behind the curtain, Humphrey's eyes bulged and he smiled aggressively.

Wilkins and Humphrey remained absolutely silent throughout the brief meeting; the two men had rehearsed their talking points before the cameras, and they reiterated the usual points about budgetary discipline and the difficulties of the shutdown and the need for flexibility, but also the importance of standing on core principles. Nothing seemed to change, but when the two men rose from the table, Stephanopoulos's gait was different: cheerier and excited.

When no sound had been heard for a solid minute, the pair of agency employees emerged from behind the curtains and hastily strode toward the door they entered.

In the Senate hallway, relieved their eavesdropping stunt hadn't triggered a visit from the U.S. Capitol Police, Humphrey was like a teakettle ready to boil over.

"Unbelievable!" Humphrey was giddy.

"I can't believe I just stole one of Bob Dole's cookies."

"Forget the cookies!" Humphrey ecstatically cried. "They're going to fold! This will be over by January!"

"Wait, just so Dole can get to New Hampshire?" Wilkins asked.

"Precisely! He can't afford to wait! The budget fight going into the New Year would interfere with Dole's chances in the primary! This is the biggest budget brinkmanship in generations, and the leader of the Republicans in the Senate just told a leading negotiator for the Democrats that he has to accept whatever's on the table at the end of the year. He just revealed his whole hand to Stephanopoulos!" He shook his head, laughed, and then laughed some more. "We're saved by Dole's ambition!"

"I can't believe what you're saying," Wilkins said, cheered but almost afraid to believe. "Why did he do that? Is he really sick of the budget showdown and looking for a way out, or did he just inadvertently blurt out the one thing he couldn't afford to reveal?"

"Does it matter?" laughed Humphrey. "Either way, the negotiations are effectively over. In a fight like this, the first side that splinters ends up conceding. Dole just told Stephanopoulos the precise date that the Republicans will give up."

They walked down the hall, privy to a joyful secret.

"Wilkins . . . remind me to touch base with Congressman Bader early next year."

5

MARCH 1996
U.S. National Debt: $5.11 trillion
Budget, USDA Agency of Invasive Species: $125.9 million

They met, month after month, meeting after meeting. Each time, Agency of Invasive Species Assistant Administrative Director Jack Wilkins tried to explain to Ava Summers, the twenty-four-year-old who somehow had become the driving force behind a massively ambitious plan to expand and revamp the agency's nascent presence on the World Wide Web, just how complicated the creation of Weed.gov would become.

It was surprisingly difficult. The inoculations of patience and lowered expectations just wouldn't take hold within her bloodstream.

"It's like the Stations of the Cross," Wilkins blurted out before realizing that the fishnet-clad woman in front of him could very well be Wiccan or something and he may have just created a workplace environment that reeked of religious intolerance in the eyes of an opportunistic litigator.

"The what?"

"Er, forget that," Wilkins said. "The bottom line is we have to go person to person, office to office, and get a lot of people to sign off on this before we even begin purchasing the equipment to make this happen."

"I like it, you like it, Humphrey likes it, and even the Speaker of the House liked it," she rolled her eyes. "You would think that would be enough."

"As you're rapidly learning, if somebody doesn't get a chance to weigh in, they'll get their noses out of joint, and there are about a million ways for them to delay or louse up a project they feel like they've been ignored on," Wilkins warned, picking up a list he had composed. "Tech, the Ag Sec, the deputy assistant administrative director for international programs, the deputy assistant administrative director for domestic programs, who will want to at least give the branch offices a chance for input. . . . At the very least, you'll have to send a memo to all of our agency liaisons. They'll probably ignore it, but you don't want this project to get halfway done and then have somebody screaming that they would have red-flagged some issue if they had been told at the beginning."

"Oh, this is my baby," Ava said with just a bit of pugnacity. "There aren't going to be any issues."

"There'll be issues. There are always issues." He liked Ava a lot, admiring her relentless enthusiasm for all of her ideas—a lot like he remembered from that first job in the Carter White House. Of course, she would learn, he concluded.

Ava had not liked anything she had been hearing from anyone within the agency since the Gingrich meeting more than a year ago. She shook her head, marveling that the meetings, proposal memos, response memos, and assorted paperwork had been circulating for so long, and that her vision was no closer to getting off sheets of paper and into electronic reality. Generally the meetings involved getting a lot of people together in the conference room, a lot of droning, a realization that some other office should be involved as well, and an agreement to reach out to that group, see what they say, and convene another meeting after that.

The Department of Agriculture already had a Web site; it featured a small photo of the building, a mailing address, the main switchboard phone number, and a lone e-mail address. Visits were few; it took thirty seconds to load up the page, and users, paying by the hour, tended not to find a visit worth the expense. Ava described what currently existed as the Wright Brothers' Glider; what she envisioned she compared to the Concorde, after Humphrey had told her to stop comparing it to the Space Shuttle.

"Our partners at NASA will feel threatened that we're encroaching upon their turf," he warned.

The tech guys—and the tech department was almost entirely guys—greeted her proposal with a series of sighs, groans, "maybes," and poorly hidden expressions of disinterest. Their pallid skin seemed to radiate the antimatter to her enthusiasm. Her least successful initial meeting came with a group of tech guys who worked in the Agriculture building's basement and were nicknamed "the Mole People."

"We've said we really prefer DOS for this kind of stuff," said one bespectacled guy who Ava had never seen before. She imagined he crawled out from a nest he had made out of old beige computer equipment in one of the basement's corners.

"Guys . . . how we do these things *changes*," she said, trying to not lose her temper, burst into tears, or fly off the handle. "My first experience with computers was the little triangle turtle in LOGO, but I learned to let him go years ago."

One of the older guys flipped through every page of her memo and plan with a wince.

"We went through this a few years ago. . . . We ran into all kinds of bugs with CompuServe and Prodigy," he said. "The data we collect is going to be a real pain to put into any kind of a database that can be displayed on the World Wide Web. . . . I'm not really sure this is going to be worth the effort."

"*Adam Humphrey* wants this done," Ava said, having learned that his name seemed to light a bit of a fire under people in the right circumstances. But his name didn't seem to have any magic down here in the basement. Ava wondered if she should have just translated her proposal into binary code directly.

In her cubicle, Ava put up a small marker board with the words "I don't get it" scrawled across the top; as a joke, she put a check mark every time she heard it from someone from whom she needed help:

"I DON'T GET IT"

April
✓ ✓ ✓

May
✓ ✓ ✓ ✓ ✓

June
✓ ✓ ✓ ✓

July
✓ ✓ ✓ ✓ ✓ ✓ ✓ ✓

By August she had run out of space. By September she stopped, because the joke was old and her coworkers' disinterest in seeing the project to fruition was no longer fun.

. . .

Of course, if the Mole People resided in subterranean caverns, the lawyers lived below them in Hades.

Ava was convinced that despite his sufficiently polite manners, Agency of Invasive Species General Counsel John Lin could make flowers wilt in his presence.

There was almost nothing outwardly nasty or hostile about Lin; he was professional, even-tempered, very smart, exceptionally diligent, a third-generation Chinese-American from San Francisco who attended Berkeley undergrad and met Humphrey when he was at Georgetown Law. Humphrey adored him, or at least he generated as much affection as anyone saw within the agency.

To Ava, the man was an endless fountain of bad news. The world of a lawyer was all about protecting his client from litigation from other lawyers, and of course, everything in American life was becoming a potential lawsuit; Lin adjusted to the ever-changing legal scene with what might be described as all-encompassing strategic paranoia. When the agency had been dragged, kicking and screaming, into the use of e-mail, Lin had written the longest standard legal confidentiality disclaimer in the entire federal government.

He had responded to Ava's proposal for Weed.gov with a fourteen-page memo that was at least eight pages of impenetrable legalese, but that Ava had no problem grasping the gist: about a hundred variations of "no."

Lin didn't like the idea of giving too many people access to the system. He was terrified of security risks, proprietary information risks, sensitive information risks, misinterpretation risks, and risk management risks. He wanted a thorough, detailed review process to evaluate every piece of information distributed by the agency to the public . . . which was more or less exactly what Weed.gov was supposed to escape.

Frequently when Ava would question one of his objections, Lin would remove his glasses, rub the bridge of his nose, and say with a sigh, "I'm afraid you're overlooking some very significant liability issues." He would then cite the case of *Somebody vs. Somebody* that to Ava sounded completely irrelevant to her Web site, and describe how in that case, somebody had done something that Lin insisted was precisely like what she was proposing, and that not only did the other somebody lose the case, but that the lawsuit decision had opened up a black hole underneath the defendant institution and said institution was sucked into the inky maw, never to be heard from again.

Every e-mail, every memo, every meeting with Lin was a variation of the same. Ava suspected that Lin would be very happy in a world of perpetually locked doors where no one ever interacted with each other, outside of e-mails with lengthy standard legal confidentiality disclaimers.

. . .

"You guys look like you've been whipped by dogs," Jamie said, realizing a moment later that she didn't really know precisely what that metaphor meant.

She had picked this week's happy hour destination, a cheery, yellow-walled Latin place called Gabriel at 2121 P Street, which offered free tapas during happy hour and promised sangria by the pitcher. Ava wondered if this week's sorrow-drowning might require tapping the national Strategic Sangria Reserve.

"I am starting to really understand why postal workers go on shooting rampages," Ava began. She laid out her latest ordeals in getting anyone to really move, to make Weed.gov an actual priority; it seemed like when people weren't nitpicking or criticizing Ava's baby, they were sleepwalking through the motions needed to bring it to fruition.

"If I'm lucky, I'll have this done by my retirement," Ava said, before emptying her sangria glass.

"Then maybe my triumphant pinnacle of my career will be writing the press release," quipped Lisa. "When I came here, I thought I would be dealing the *New York Times*, the *Washington Post, George* magazine—you know, the *real* news publications—but not only does absolutely nothing this agency do ever get noticed by anybody, or does anybody care about anything we do, but I don't even get to handle the few calls we do get. They're mostly from agricultural trade publications, and my boss handles them, and he's absolutely terrible at them. He never says anything. His answers go on and on, with this, like, fog of words, and when I read his quotes they've been cut down to nothing. Like: 'We are monitoring the developments in this area and are confident that our responses will be sufficiently adaptive.' Or something like that, which could mean anything. The only media calls I ever deal with are from some stupid tiny little wire service that has all of its reporters read the *Federal Register* every morning."

"Event-planning must be the best job, Jamie," Ava said, plopping back in her chair. "You get to plan trips and conferences for the senior staff. As the only one of us whose job doesn't suck our souls out through our eyeballs every day, I think you should buy the next pitcher."

Jamie looked down at the table for a second.

"This week I got a call from the Inspector General's office."

"Next round's on me," Lisa said, as Ava shot up into an upright posture.

. . .

Two days earlier, with great trepidation, Jamie poked her head into Humphrey's office.

"The Inspector General's office just called."

"What did he want?" Humphrey asked. He almost fooled her into thinking he wasn't unnerved by those words.

Suddenly the intercom on his desk beeped to life. His secretary, Carla, announced that it was USDA Inspector General Demetrius Palmer on the line.

Humphrey picked up the boxy receiver. "Mr. Palmer! How do you do?" The voice on the other end was not nearly so warm. "Travel records for the past four years? Absolutely."

. . .

Shortly after sending over the records, Humphrey asked for a meeting with the recently appointed Inspector General Palmer.

The first available meeting time was a week later. Humphrey crossed the massive building and arrived early. Humphrey didn't know much about Palmer, but he instinctively perceived all inspectors general as potential adversaries.

Palmer was already one of President Clinton's favorites, starting in the Department of Commerce and finding, in short order, a web of egregious contractor overcharging. He had been appointed to the Department of Agriculture IG spot a few months ago.

Humphrey had taught Wilkins to consider OIG staff the way cops considered internal affairs snoops in their precincts. He would have sneeringly labeled them the "rat squad," but that nickname had already been taken by the agency's invasive rodent management and abatement working group.

Palmer's office suite was quiet, diligent, not a thing out of place. The secretary said Palmer was running late, and when the tall, black, perfectly groomed lawyer emerged from his office several minutes later, he offered Humphrey an apology that didn't seem apologetic at all.

They entered Palmer's office, where the walls were covered with awards, a photo of him with the president here, a photo with Janet Reno there. Palmer had already laid out a variety of documents and spreadsheets on his desk.

"I'll get straight to it, Humphrey," Palmer began. "The travel budget for your agency's senior staff is . . . considerable."

"Well considered, I would argue," he said with a smile. Palmer didn't smile back. Instead, he simply looked through a series of photocopied records where he had marked certain lines with adhesive notes.

"Last April, University of Tokyo. Spain, early May, International Organization for Biological Control of Noxious Animals and Plants. June, Victoria, British Columbia, Society for Ecological Restoration. August, International Workshop on Grapevine Trunk Diseases, Valencia, Spain. September, New Zealand Biosecurity Institute's Seminar, Wairakei Resort Hotel, Taupo, New Zealand."

He removed his glasses.

"I've seen diplomats who rack up fewer frequent flyer miles than you, Humphrey," Palmer said, as serious as the end of happy hour.

"Mr. Palmer, I admit, I'm a bit surprised that you find this to be an issue," Humphrey began. "The very name of our agency explains the necessity of this travel. 'Invasive,' as in 'invading,' as in 'from somewhere else.' If we could do all of our work from this building, we would be happy to. But our work involves weeds and pollen-spreading insects and all of God's creation coming across our borders from somewhere else—in an era of international trade and air travel, oftentimes someplace quite far away—and thus our mission requires us to develop working relationships with experts from all around the globe."

"I also notice that the conferences you host here in America are . . . pretty expensive by government standards. And I can't help but notice they're in . . . nice destinations: Miami, Las Vegas, San Diego, Honolulu. Warm weather, winter dates. A suspicious mind might look at these conferences as taxpayer-funded vacations for you and your staff."

Humphrey's insincere smile dropped like a shattered window. He began to return fire, drawing his sarcasm as if it were a sheathed knife.

"We work with *farmers*, Mr. Palmer, and you'll find that many of us do this here at the Department of *Agriculture*. Farmers tend to be *busy* in the spring, summer, and autumn months. Something about *planting*, growing, and harvesting *crops*. For some *strange* reason, they seem to have the most time to attend a conference in the winter months. Perhaps you could uncover those secrets with an extensive investigation. Besides, if you examine all of our records, you'll see we hold regional conferences at other times of the year in plenty of other cities. We always hold one in Manchester, New Hampshire, usually in late September or early October—"

"Fall foliage season."

"New Orleans in late winter . . ."

"Mardi Gras."

"Our end-of-the-year meeting in Manhattan."

"Christmas at Rockefeller Center."

Palmer smelled a snow job.

"Nice hotels, too, Humphrey."

"Mr. Palmer, just who do you think we invite to these conferences? Our ability to achieve our mission depends greatly upon the quality of the expertise we draw upon. If I'm going to ask the top biologists and agricultural science professors from Oxford University, Kyoto University, McGill, Edinburgh, Australian National, or Singapore to get on a plane for ten hours and spend time briefing and updating our top agricultural minds on their latest findings, I had better put them up at a nice hotel with fun things to do after hours. Otherwise, they won't come. Perhaps you would prefer I hold it at the Holiday Inn outside Dulles Airport?"

Palmer was unmoved. "Of course, in the process, you and your senior staff end up staying at the government per diem rate at these luxury resorts."

"You will find every figure in order, every *i* dotted, every *t* crossed," Humphrey hissed indignantly.

"It's not just the figures, Mr. Humphrey, it's the frequency of the travel and the overall expense of the conferences. Look, my job is not just to sniff out misconduct, fraud, theft, waste, and so on. It's also to flag circumstances that could become problems down the road. If any of this ended up on the front page of the *Washington Post*, you would be getting a lot of grief. And at that point, it might be too late to do anything."

Humphrey detected a not-so-veiled threat.

"Will you be assembling an official report on this?"

"Would that . . . worry you, Mr. Humphrey?"

"I would merely like time to assemble . . . all of the relevant information. To help give you a full picture of our work," his insincere smile returned.

. . .

Humphrey immediately summoned Wilkins and Jamie to his office, and instructed Carla they were not to be disturbed.

Within the office, Wilkins had gone from his usual trepidation to anger.

"I cannot believe this!" Wilkins fumed again, holding a Diet Coke against his forehead. "We finally get the Hill calmed down, and now our own IG is breathing down our necks?"

"Think of all the hours we wasted in this effort to sniff out wastes of money," Humphrey sighed.

"You're sure he was threatening to leak it to the *Washington Post*?" Jamie asked.

Humphrey reviewed the notes he had written down immediately after the meeting.

"He had marked the conference spending that interested him in his spreadsheets with adhesive notes, but did not have anything written down. That, my dear Ms. Caro, is the key moment in all this. Perhaps that or the moment his fingertip hits the button to 'save document.' Once it gets written down on paper—or screen—it can get printed, photocopied, passed around, shown, read, repeated . . . at that point, we're chasing paper airplanes all around any possible connection between this Department and anyone with access to a printing press. Inspectors General exist to expose problems. If they don't expose problems, they don't feel like they're doing their job." He looked over his own copy of the travel records. "This is the choke point, the moment where we can deter all manner of headaches from this. If we can somehow instantly persuade him that all of this travel is so justified, so natural, so needed, that questioning it would be stirring up a hornet's nest for himself . . ."

Wilkins drank down his soda. "Let's find some other office to distract him. Find some other juicier example of potential waste for him to shine a spotlight on."

"No good comes from federal agencies and offices turning on each other," Humphrey said curtly. "No, we need to get him to see what we do as absolutely imperative . . ."

He thought for several moments, then burst into activity: "Wilkins, this agency has been tracking and mitigating weed outbreaks in just about every state for nearly twenty years. It is time we laid out for him every detail of every action we've taken that has ever required travel."

. . .

For nine straight days, Agency of Invasive Species staff appeared in the doorway of the Inspector General's office, pulling hand-carts full of cardboard boxes, packed to the gills with photo-copied documents and receipts and records and every other conceivable piece of paperwork. They came several times during a day. Palmer's secretary faced the increasingly frequent question, "Where do you want these?" with steadily increasing dread.

Throughout the Department of Agriculture's offices, staffers wondered why their previous extra copier and printer toner had disappeared. The agency had actually worn out its photo-copier, and staffers were now wandering into other offices just to use their photocopier.

Palmer noticed that document boxes were starting to line the walkways between cubicles. "There must be some mistake," he told the hapless intern lugging the boxes around. "I'm only reviewing travel for the past four years."

The intern checked a note. "Yeah, Mr. Humphrey said you might ask that. He said, let me see here—these are records for trips that were planned within the preceding physical year—"

"Fiscal year," Palmer corrected.

"Oh yeah. Previous fisk-able year, but occurred in the period under review. Also, he said some of the trips from four years ago were follow-up investigations to events in the years before those, so he's sending the records for those, too."

"I don't need those records," Palmer sighed.

"He told me that if I didn't get these to you I could get in big trouble."

Palmer sighed. "Fine."

. . .

Two weeks later, Humphrey had requested another meeting with Inspector General Palmer. The deluge of records continued unabated, and Office of the Inspector General staffers now grimly joked they were preparing to build an Ark.

Humphrey attempted to stride confidently into Palmer's office, but found the door could not open the entire way, banging up against a stack of document boxes. Wilkins joined him this time, but instead of carrying his usual briefcase, Wilkins gingerly held a plastic carrying case with opaque sides. He offered Palmer's secretary a thoroughly unconvincing smile, but she merely skeptically measured him and his mysterious case, wondering why he was handling it like it was a nuclear bomb.

"Mr. Palmer, I appreciate you taking the time to see me again," Humphrey began as he settled into his chair, and pushed it, ever so slightly, about two inches further away from Palmer's desk. "This is our assistant administrative director, Jack Wilkins. Let me begin with apologies; our last meeting took a much more combative tone than warranted. I failed to appreciate the diligence and drive you bring to your mission, and understand that in all of this, you're merely doing your duty."

"I appreciate that, Humphrey, and I have to say you've gone way beyond what I asked in turning over documentation," Palmer nodded. "In fact, I don't think we're going to need—"

"Before you go any further, Mr. Palmer, permit me to offer a second apology, for assuming you were dismissing the importance of our work. Sometimes I forget how our efforts can seem so antiseptic, abstract, and difficult to grasp on memos and spreadsheets. People hear the 'Agency of Invasive Species' and picture space aliens or giant plant-monsters, or . . ." Humphrey paused, and watched Palmer's eyes closely. "Or plagues of locusts."

"I cannot imagine why someone would associate you with plagues," Palmer said with a straight face.

"I wanted you to see our work with your own eyes, to appreciate our need to get out into the field," Humphrey continued, getting the confirmation he had sought. "Jack has brought you a most vivid example of some of our recent important work, dealing with the crops of the Midwest. You see, up to one billion dollars in crops are lost each year from the Western corn rootworm—"

Wilkins carefully unlocked the latch and opened the lid—and a slew of black-and-yellow beetles crawled within, several attaching themselves to the lid and then starting to drop to the floor and desk.

Palmer pushed himself back in a distinctly unmasculine fashion upon the sight of the bugs.

"What . . . are those things and why did you just put them on my desk?!" Palmer asked, failing to hide the tension in his voice.

"I'm sorry, I'll get them back in here, it's just they're . . . you know, small, and pretty fast, and—damn—hang on, I'll get that guy," Wilkins removed rubber gloves and attempted to grab the bugs, failing to put the lid on quick enough to keep a few more from crawling out onto the desk.

"*Diabrotica virgifera virgifera*, scourge of the Corn Belt," Humphrey said, trying to keep his voice even but not-so-subtly inching away from them. He put a picture of the bug magnified a thousand times onto the desk; up close, the mandibles, horns, and spiky legs resembled the radioactive giant ants of the 1950s sci-fi Cold War nuclear monster thriller *Them!*

"That's fine, Humphrey, I don't need them on my desk!" Palmer said, grabbing a paper and starting to roll it up for a swat.

"Do be careful, Mr. Palmer, I understand these beetles can be aggressive when they feel provoked or threatened, with stings and bites," Humphrey cautioned, inching back again. It wasn't really true, Humphrey knew; the bugs were harmless to humans, but Palmer appeared to be rapidly succumbing to a medical condition technically diagnosed as the heebie-jeebies.

"Now, in the crate marked 3A-6B, you'll find a series of records involving our travel to Chicago, Illinois, and Kansas City, Missouri, in the aftermath of infestations of this particular species." Humphrey looked around, trying to ignore the crawling beetles in front of him, noticing that a good half-dozen crates were taking up space in Palmer's office. "Do you have those records handy?"

Humphrey, Wilkins, and Jamie had sent constant messages to Palmer lamenting that they had tried to send the files in reverse chronological order, but also sending them as they found them to avoid concerns that any particular documents were being withheld. To clarify which records were in which box, they devised an unnecessarily complicated alphanumeric system that left every box sounding like a droid from *Star Wars*. Palmer's staff had found going through the files an enormous ordeal, often wondering how their life's twists and turns had left them examining a photocopy of a receipt for a sandwich purchase from O'Hare Airport in 1992.

"Three what? Look, it's going to take me a while to dig out— I'm sorry, you said these bugs bite when they feel provoked?"

"That's what the literature says," Wilkins shrugged, "but the odds of any of us having an allergic reaction are pretty small, as I understand it."

Palmer shifted his chair as far back as it could go. "Allergic?"

"Yes, well, the beetle is particularly relevant to our battle against the weed menace, as it is also a common carrier of ragweed pollen—"

"I'm allergic to ragweed!" growled Palmer, eyes glaring.

He noticed one of the beetles crawling on the armrest of his chair, and Palmer leaped out, stumbling and throwing himself into an adjacent metal filing cabinet.

"GET THESE"—many more expletives—"OUT OF MY OFFICE NOW, HUMPHREY!"

"Absolutely, sir, but first I'd just like to point out that these insects are an example of why my senior staff may attend biological research conferences that don't seem directly applicable to our effort against weeds. You see, today I wanted to ensure that the importance of our work is clarif—"

"OUT! NOW! HUMPHREY!" The inspector general's eyeballs seemed disturbingly close to bulging out of their sockets.

"Of course, my friend," Humphrey smiled. "Wilkins." He looked a bit unnerved as one of the larger beetles began crawling across the desk toward him. He cleared his throat uncomfortably. "Wilkins!"

"Working on it!"

Finally the butterfly net dislodged itself from the satchel.

"DO YOU HEAR HISSING?"

. . .

The remainder of the meeting was . . . brief. Once the bugs had been netted and redeposited into the plastic crate, Palmer practically pushed them out the door.

"So, I trust your upcoming report—if any—will reflect the importance of the invasive species threats that we assess and mitigate?" Humphrey asked in a jovial tone that masked the men's near–nervous breakdown after the Battle of the Bugs. "You'll emphasize that while our travel and conference budget may seem high to the untrained eye, they represent a wise and necessary investment in the agency that is, after all, all that stands between us and these little buggers—"

"Oh, you've made that abundantly clear, Humphrey," Palmer fumed, feeling the back of his neck, unsure if his periodic sensation of tiny little legs crawling on him was psychosomatic. "Listen, never bring anything with more than two legs into my office again. In fact, never come into my office again."

"As you wish, Mr. Palmer, but know that my staff and I are always at your service," Humphrey said with a beaming smile, quite confident that the Inspector General wanted nothing to do with Humphrey and his agency ever again.

They departed the office suite and stood outside the hallway. Humphrey could not quite stifle a smirk.

"Okay, it worked," Wilkins admitted. "It worked terrifically, but I still think there had to be an easier way to get Palmer off our backs than renting a box of beetles and making me play Marlin Perkins to the mini-Mothras here."

"Oh, Jack," Humphrey chuckled, pressing the elevator button. "You've been with me long enough to understand my belief in the influential power of the sudden, unexpected, visceral reaction. We could have used tiny bugs, but I doubt that would have . . . stirred the heart of Palmer in the way we desired. He'll probably never come near our office again!" He stifled a bit of louder laughter, then noticed Wilkins was looking at his plastic case quite intensely.

"What, are you growing attached to them now?"

Wilkins looked up at Humphrey with a look of barely repressed horror. "I'm pretty sure we left a bunch of them in there."

The two exchanged an unnerved look, glanced back at the door to Palmer's office suite and then at each other again.

"Let's take the stairs."

DECEMBER 1997
U.S. National Debt: $5.49 trillion
Budget, USDA Agency of Invasive Species: $146.9 million

Nick Bader's wife, Anne, was not enjoying life as a congressional spouse.

They were packing up a portion of their house; she and their three children had decided to relocate from Bucks County, Pennsylvania, to McLean, Virginia. Nick Bader found that every congressman lived in two places simultaneously, both in Washington and in their home district. Miss a vote and the opposition would claim you're neglecting your duties; spend the weekends in Washington and you were accused of going native and forgetting the folks back home. Bader suspected that very few constituents really cared where he was; some folks just wanted something to complain about.

Anne Bader had been initially excited about public life—she spoke at a few campaign events, and when her husband won, she felt a quiet thrill that the people of this Pennsylvania congressional district seemed to see the greatness she saw in him. But within a year, she wanted the voters to go away and let her and their children live a normal life. Neighbors and acquaintances shared any and all complaints about government at any level, with the unspoken assumption that her husband would be able to do something about it. Every new friend had to be regarded with a certain unspoken suspicion; sudden acts of kindness often seemed to come with a subsequent request for a favor. Suddenly, every new friendly face had to be treated warily.

In 1996 Bader won reelection fairly handily, and Anne thought that the stressful transition to life in the public spotlight would ease. Nick Bader became a slightly less perpetually stressed husband and father, and his temperamental outbursts occurred less frequently, but she sensed a low-boil frustration within him.

That night, after all the packing, lying in bed in the dark and dreading the partial move the next day—the Baders intended to keep the house in Bucks County as his legal residence—Nick

Bader let out that frustration, in a quiet whisper rather than the burst of anger Anne expected.

"I'm not sure I'm ever going to do what I thought I was meant to do," he said quietly. "A lot of days I feel like I'm talking to myself, or to an empty chamber. My bills go nowhere. I don't feel like anybody really listens to me. We didn't really cut much of anything our first year, didn't happen the second year, and it's not looking that good in this year or next," he sighed.

"You're fighting the good fight," she said, brushing his head. "That's all anyone can ask of you—including yourself."

"At least Sisyphus managed to move the rock," he continued. "Everyone who comes to Washington intending to cut the government comes with some other goal as well—defense, abortion, schools, whatever. And everyone who likes the government the way it is has gotten very, very skilled at figuring out how to get us to focus on the other stuff."

"The first day I saw you at Princeton, you were wearing glasses and a leather jacket, and you were arguing with some College Republican about Nixon—something about . . ."

"Price controls," Bader recalled with a smile. "I was trying to get that my-party-can-do-no-wrong dweeb—God, what was his name?—to grasp that our guy had just unilaterally decided that the government can freeze wages for everyone in the country."

"Anyway, I kind of knew who you were, but I remember thinking—that guy's going to get things done." She kissed him on the cheek. "I still believe in that man."

She went to sleep, and Nick Bader slept a bit better than he had the previous few nights.

6

FEBRUARY 1998
U.S. National Debt: $5.52 trillion
Budget, USDA Agency of Invasive Species: $148.7 million

As administrative director, Adam Humphrey was deeply concerned about the office's sexual harassment management policies. Wilkins didn't see what the big deal was.

"After the whole Anita Hill thing, we set up the system to run the annual seminars—we haven't had any serious complaints. That guy Tom, the analyst, waited until the cute one finished her internship before he asked her out."

"Jack, that was before the entire city and country heard that the president had been . . . *with* an intern."

"Oh, he didn't do it!" scoffed Wilkins. "Probably."

Humphrey shot him a witheringly disappointed look.

"Jack, I don't gamble, but if I did, I would bet on the credibility of any allegation of sexual conduct between the president and a young lady. No matter what woman, inside or outside the administration, I would always bet that the claim is true. Do you know why?"

"Illuminate me, Adam."

"Because it would be a sound long-term investment strategy!" Humphrey barked with sarcasm. "Sure, periodically, I would lose the bet, but in the long term, the number of women who would voluntarily expose themselves to ridicule over their sex life for the sake of a false allegation to discredit a hated politician is far fewer than the number of women who would only find that price worth paying in the name of exposing the truth."

Wilkins shook his head. "Adam, your view of women's unwillingness to lie isn't just dated, it's carbon-dated."

"Chivalrous," Humphrey corrected. "Either way, the emerging scandal guarantees that the preeminent topic of discussion for everyone in the entire agency in every office, both here and in the field, will be sex. Sex between bosses and subordinates, sex between married people and unmarried people, sex in the office, sex on the phone . . ."

"Ah, I get it. Way too easy for someone to say something and offend someone, huh?"

"At the very least!" Humphrey harrumphed. "Jack, now that the president of the United States has started enjoying the intern pool as his own personal harem, how many other men in our agency will contemplate the same approach to their coworkers?"

"Okay, I see where you're going with this," Wilkins nodded. "You're afraid the old rule of, 'Don't shi—er, make a mess where you eat' is going to fall by the wayside."

Humphrey gave him a knowing glance. "The modern workplace puts men and women into close quarters for long periods of time. Throw in stress and deadlines, the need to work as a team, the desire for team camaraderie, after-hours happy hour trips, business travel, and the natural inclinations of men and women for . . . affection and contact and . . . things will happen. If I could permit these adult acts to be sorted out by adults, I would be happy. But any one of these interactions could result in a messy lawsuit or bad publicity."

"Lin's been talking to you, hasn't he?" Wilkins asked, recognizing the telltale panic of the agency's general counsel John Lin, the most lawsuit-averse lawyer to walk the earth.

"I have a legal duty to make sure that there is a well-posted set of rules and regulations indicating how men and women should interact with each other at this agency!" said an agitated Humphrey.

. . .

Seeking out the most groundbreaking and far-reaching approach to mitigating sexual confusion, Humphrey turned to a policy adopted a few years earlier by Antioch College:

1. For the purpose of this policy, "consent" shall be defined as follows: the act of willingly and verbally agreeing to engage in specific sexual contact or conduct.

2. If sexual contact and/or conduct is not mutually and simultaneously initiated, then the person who initiates sexual contact/conduct is responsible for getting the verbal consent of the other individual(s) involved.

Ava, Jamie, and Lisa found it all quite laughable.

For a few weeks, every routine request or interaction prompted a response of, "Are you initiating sexual contact or conduct with me?"

3. Obtaining consent is an on-going process in any sexual interaction. Verbal consent should be obtained with each new level of physical and/or sexual contact/conduct in any given interaction, regardless of who initiates it. Asking "Do you want to have sex with me?" is not enough. The request for consent must be specific to each act.

"Dammit, Lisa, when we were in the copy room, I specifically indicated that I granted consent to second base and no further!" Ava shouted loudly across the cubicles. "I did not give any signal to steal third!"

4. The person with whom sexual contact/conduct is initiated is responsible to express verbally and/or physically her/his willingness or lack of willingness when reasonably possible.

"When reasonably possible?" Jamie giggled.

"Remember, it's rude to talk when your mouth is full!" roared Ava.

Humphrey was mortified to learn that his policy designed to prevent and deter sexual comments had ensured that dozens of agency employees took the opportunity to make suggestive jokes about each other, in the name of mocking the policy, for the entire day. He closed his office door and hoped nothing would happen.

JUNE 1998

"Would you ever sleep with your boss?" Ava asked.

"That's a completely different question from whether I would ever sleep with Bill Clinton," Lisa replied. "And if it meant the president's golfing buddies would start trying to find me a better job, that would be a hell of an afterglow."

Lisa's love life had been . . . dissatisfying in recent years.

"This town doesn't have that many real men, outside of the military," she said after a gulp. Jamie had been dating a handsome Marine recently, and the new couple seemed quite happy.

"No, that's not true. It just attracts a particular type, and you have to know what you're getting," Ava said. "You can develop your brain, or you can develop your body, and it's very hard to develop both. Here, most of the guys have developed their brains. They're very career focused. They don't dress spectacularly well, but they wear dark suits and ties most days. They don't need to stand out, they don't want to stand out too much, and they're probably going to get in trouble if they stand out too much."

"Sometimes I wonder if I should move somewhere else," Lisa sighed. "Someplace . . . real."

"No, Ava's right, here you get guys working crazy hours on the Hill and checking their pagers and catching their friends on C-SPAN," Jamie chimed in. "But the culture in D.C. weeds out a lot of other varieties of jerk. Back home in Miami, you get people who want to look good. It's very, very important to them. They work out constantly. They wear almost nothing on the beach. They wear almost nothing off the beach. The women wear higher heels, shorter skirts—all the outfits that we get those tsk-tsk looks for here in Washington are, like, formal wear in Miami."

"New York's kinda the same," Ava replied. "Every time I go back home to visit my folks I get culture shock over cleavage and tight jeans and glossy lipstick. I know they call me 'Fishnets Girl,' but compared to Manhattan, I'm wearing a hijab." She shrugged. "Sometimes I wonder who I'm dressing for. Who is here? When did this place become full of . . . bores?"

"That's not true," Jamie said, feeling a bit of local pride burning through her margarita buzz. "Washington has culture. There's Georgetown."

"Old money," Ava said with a roll of her eyes. "WASPs lining up their antiques in their bay windows for the gawking tourists who wander up from M Street."

"Dupont Circle."

"Gay."

"Adams Morgan."

"Hipster bike messenger working on his one-act play about women in Bosnia."

"That was just one guy!" laughed Jamie. "And he was mature compared to that guy who wanted to watch *The Muppet Movie* on his birthday."

"So if half the guys around here take themselves way too seriously, and the other half have serious cases of arrested development, it's not surprising that some women our age turn to . . . more mature men as an option," Lisa said, wondering if either of her friends would wonder if she had some particular more mature man in mind.

But neither took the bait, and Ava began analyzing Washington's social mores as though they were a giant complicated system or machine: "This town has more almost-celebrities per capita than . . . like, Nashville or Hollywood. The assistant undersecretary of whatever, or the head of Concerned Americans for American Concerns, or the Washington Bureau Chief of the *Nowhere Times-Herald*. Almost all of the celebrities are married, and aren't supposed to be looking. Everybody's worried about reputation; everybody's worried that they could get caught banging somebody on the photocopier after hours. Of course, in this situation, once there are impossibly dire consequences for doing that, all anybody can think about is banging the object of their desire on the photocopier after hours."

They laughed and ordered another round.

"What was that thing Henry Kissinger said?" Lisa asked.

Jamie wrinkled her nose. " 'South America is a dagger pointed straight at the heart of Antarctica'?"

"No, no—'Power is the ultimate aphrodisiac.' A lot of people in Washington work really hard to get power. Budgetary power, lawmaking power, influential power, power to put messages in the press, the power of connections—this is the only city where men brag to women about how they've got a great big, thick . . . Rolodex," Lisa said, spurring another round of giggles. "Think about how much they sacrifice for it—the degrees from the top schools, the crappy internships, the sucking up to the boss, the long hours."

"Sometimes they'll marry a philanderer and pretend they don't know just to be First Lady," quipped Ava.

"Sounds sad," Jamie said, and then she realized her assessment applied to both their amateur psychoanalysis of Hillary Clinton and the power-focused men Lisa described.

"So lots of the people here don't have the looks," Lisa continued. "They've spent their youth working, but now they reach some perch where they've got a little prestige. Nice office, nice watch. And every summer we get *skinterns*, who don't know how to dress and who come around the office half naked, showcasing their just-past-teenage bodies. It's kind of amazing there aren't midsummer pagan orgies."

"The Christian Coalition would object," Jamie said.

Ava found the romantic recon assessment bleak. "So you're saying we're destined to become the cute young playthings of some older, more successful man."

"Oh, no!" Lisa laughed confidently. "You've heard about those women senators on the Hill with their much younger, hunkier drivers. We can get our own boy toys."

AUGUST 1998

After President Clinton's grand jury testimony, calls for impeachment mounted. Upon their return from the August recess, the House Republicans met in one of the Capitol's cavernous conference rooms, with a few joining via conference call. Tom DeLay had characterized the upcoming effort to impeach Clinton as "the most important thing I do in my political career" and gave his staff and colleagues an ultimatum: "Dedicate yourselves to it or leave."

Bader felt torn.

He knew he would probably end up voting for impeachment; the president's judgment was just too reckless.

To flash her thong at the president of the United States in his workplace, Monica Lewinsky had to be at least a little crazy. Perhaps forgivably crazy, as crushes, love, and lust drive us to do mad things, Bader thought. But Bill Clinton should have— had to have—known better. He was the grownup. If you don't have sufficient impulse control to avoid doing *that* for eight years, don't run for two terms as president.

For Bader, the most revelatory point of the gargantuan Starr report came in just one line from a transcript of a call between Lewinsky and Linda Tripp. Lewinsky told her that Clinton had said, "I have an empty life except for my work."

There was no way to be certain if Lewinsky was quoting Clinton verbatim or even accurately, but she would have little reason to lie, and didn't know she was being recorded. Bader could picture Clinton saying it. Bader could picture Clinton thinking it and believing it. He shuddered when he thought of Hillary and Chelsea reading those words. Putting aside any of the complications of the Clintons' marriage, what the hell was wrong with this man that he would tell his mistress that his child meant nothing to him?

Impeach the bastard, Bader concluded.

BUT . . . he hadn't come to Washington to do that. His battle plans to cut the bureaucracy to the bone were gathering dust. As emotionally satisfying as it would be to go after Clinton, he knew that pursuing impeachment meant jumping down the rabbit hole, with no sense of how long the journey would take, where it would end, or how he and his colleagues would emerge when it was all over.

The Republicans in the conference room appeared increasingly set on pursuing impeachment as the meeting dragged on.

Finally, Bader spoke up. "Look, guys, isn't anybody worried that if we start doing this, it takes over our entire agenda for the foreseeable future? I mean, we came here to cut government, pull up the weeds, and ever since we got our asses kicked in the shutdown, we've been afraid to get back into the ring. If Clinton's on his knees—"

He heard giggling in the back.

"Quit giggling, you're grown men! Why not take this opportunity to press the president on policy?"

"You mean let him off the hook in exchange for a few budget cuts? Are you serious, Bader?"

The room rejected the idea instantly and outright. A passionate consensus in favor of impeachment emerged, and the House Republicans exuberantly adjourned the meeting and filed out the doors.

Bader was the last one left in the room.

"Doesn't anybody want to cut the government anymore?" he asked the empty room.

7

JANUARY 1999
U.S. National Debt: $5.6 trillion
Budget, USDA Agency of Invasive Species: $162.33 million

For four years, Ava used two verbal sticks of dynamite to dislodge the obstacles facing Weed.gov: the first was, *Adam Humphrey says this is a priority.* The line's effectiveness worked in direct relation to how close the person was to Humphrey's office. It worked within the administrative staff of the Agency of Invasive Species, somewhat with other Department of Agriculture offices, and not much at all with the Mole People in the basement ... and it was useless with the agency field offices.

But the other line that worked less often than she expected was, *The Speaker of the House has personally endorsed this project as a priority.* Her coworkers often rolled their eyes, and sometimes blurted out how much they detested him. Among the federal workforce, the Speaker of the House of Representatives was surprisingly unfeared.

She hoped invoking the name of Newt Gingrich would be her sword to cut the Gordian knot of red tape; apparently her sword smith was Nerf®. And now even that was being taken from her.

He didn't even make the announcement in person: "Today I have reached a difficult personal decision. The Republican conference needs to be unified, and it is time for me to move forward where I believe I still have a significant role to play for our country and our party." Some rotund wrestling coach she had never heard of was the new Speaker.

. . .

Ava was halfway through a thoroughly miserable day when she received an e-mail from an old college classmate—technically, an old fling—Raj Chattopadhyay.

She hadn't heard from him in about two years, but out of the blue he said he would be in Washington for a couple of days and wanted to grab dinner. His e-mail signature indicated he was now 'director of management initiatives' at some company called GlobeScape in Palo Alto, California.

Booty call, Ava surmised.

But he had recommended dinner at a new place, DC Coast, and she wondered what seven years of postcollegiate life had done to old Raj.

His choice was one of the city's newest and most popular K Street restaurants, a site that celebrated the power and luxury that now surged through the avenues of the once-sleepy city.

A bronze-colored mermaid greeted patrons at the door, her breasts brazenly exposed. Giant oval mirrors sat on the walls above the tables, letting every status-minded diner know who else was there and who wasn't, and who was sitting with whom. The cuisine cost quite a bit, but seemed worth it, at least to a palate like Ava's, which had relied heavily on Pop-Tarts and bar chow.

Raj arrived, impeccably dressed—his suit was Armani, and it probably cost one of Ava's paychecks. His black, curly hair had grown a little longer, and he had a small, unobtrusive ponytail. His watch cost more than the suit.

Ava found she didn't feel hit-upon; she was pleasantly surprised to find Raj really wanted to reconnect with a long-lost friend.

"So how's life in Washington?" he asked after ordering appetizers. "You seemed very Manhattan, very NYU, so I was kind of surprised you moved here—but then I remembered you were going to save the world."

"Change the world," she corrected. "And . . . Washington sucks. So four years ago—wait, five now, I guess—right after I started, I come up with this plan to get the agency on the Internet—beyond the embarrassing single page they had at the time. Huge. Elaborate, groundbreaking, exactly what the Internet would be if you took hold of all of its potential at once— this thing is beautiful. I'm still working on it. Five years, and it is bare bones—crashes all the time, the data is out of date, nobody listens, nobody pays attention . . ." she sighed. "I'm . . . I really need to get out of here. I'm growing old here."

Raj oddly smiled. "You are completely in the wrong place. Nobody goes to Washington to change the world anymore. Washington's irrelevant. I mean, didn't the president say in some press conference that he still matters? If you have to remind people of that, you don't really matter. You want to know where the action is? Fifteen hundred square miles in California south of San Francisco."

He was beaming. Ava looked at him in a new light, admiringly, but she felt jealousy gurgling up from deep within her. She felt a need to puncture the air out of that ego.

"I figured you were soulless enough to go work on Wall Street selling junk bonds or something," she said with a raised eyebrow.

"Ha!" Raj laughed. "I love where I work. It's amazing how

few people have heard of GlobeScape, because we really are the essence of what Silicon Valley is all about. And . . . we're doing something that I think you would be very interested in."

Not a booty call after all, Ava realized.

"Go on."

"In nine months, GlobeScape plans to launch EasyFed.com, a Web portal-platform designed to provide services to help people deal with the federal government."

"Like what?"

"Well, we're going to take the traffic from the government sites . . . instead of paying your taxes online, or applying for a grant, or complaining that your Social Security check didn't arrive on time, you'll go to our site, click on what you need, fill out the data, and BOOM. Done."

"Doesn't that just create a middleman?"

"Ava . . ." Raj scoffed. "You of all people know that dealing with any part of the federal government is a pain in the ass. The sites are slow, they're down, they're poorly laid out, they're not intuitive. The beautiful thing is, once we get all of this set up, almost all of this can be automated. We just need people to build the site. Once it's done and running, the thing will run itself! Set it and forget it."

She tried to picture in her head the whole system working. "So, once I've helped build the site, what will you need me for?"

"Well, somebody needs to make sure it continues to run, and we can expand and develop it to work on new services—state governments, local governments, etcetera. This is a big project with lots of opportunities for expansion. We are talking about the largest customer base in America—everyone who has to interact with the government in any way: 270 million people."

She couldn't help herself—she admired Raj, but he had the bad habit of believing his own bull. "You're counting the kids. And you're counting the people who aren't on the Internet."

"Okay, fine. We're *only* talking about everyone on the Internet who has to interact with the government in any way. The federal government has enormous brand leverage and market share for government services"—Ava resisted the urge to burst out laughing at the nonsensical marketing doublespeak—"and so our aim with EasyFed is to take that and integrate it into our business model."

Ava felt herself growing more intrigued. "How will this EasyGov or whatever make money?"

"Eventually we'll charge usage and processing fees, like banks, but for now we're building market share. We're also contemplating Web advertising. The big deal these days is building a platform that can leverage what we call 'floating sticky eyeballs.'"

"One pop-up ad and you'll lose everyone," she warned.

"Ava, you need to get out there," Raj leaned across the table and started to close the sale. He cheerfully boasted that Silicon Valley had been the ultimate boomtown since Netscape incorporated in 1994.

"Silicon Valley is to the rest of the United States what the United States is to the rest of the world," Raj said. "You can just *feel* the electricity in the air."

"You're probably feeling the power lines giving everyone brain cancer," she said, biting down on an ice cube. "Okay . . . I'm interested. What's the next step?"

"Let's pick some dates soon for you to come out and meet some people."

She smiled a warm smile that had been all too infrequent lately. "I think I'd like that."

"I'd like that, too."

A game of footsie commenced under the table.

At the conclusion of the meal, Raj grabbed the check before Ava could even look at it.

"I've got this. This is a recruitment dinner. At GlobeScape, we don't do anything halfway. Platinum company credit cards are for old money. We have *osmium*," he said, throwing down a silvery-blue slice of plastic.

. . .

GlobeScape FedExed plane tickets to her Dupont Circle efficiency apartment. Ava took some vacation days and flew business class for the first time in her life. At the San Jose airport, Raj picked her up in a BMW that could not have been more than six months old.

"Alright, I'm impressed already," she said as they drove away from the airport.

Raj flashed a gleaming smile.

"We're just getting started," he said, kicking the car into a higher gear onto Interstate 880—the engine roared beautifully, for about twenty seconds, before the traffic ahead forced him to stop and idle.

"Everything's new out here," Raj said happily. "Except Stanford University. I thought about going there."

"You were too much of an East Coast guy, huh?"

"I'm starting to think it was a huge mistake," he said, before correcting himself. "I mean, I'm glad I met you at NYU, and things turned out fine. But I think we were a couple of oddballs who didn't fit in."

"I always thought the city was big enough for everybody," she said.

Until moving to Washington, Ava had considered herself a New Yorker in spirit. For much of her childhood, her father worked in midtown Manhattan in the production department of a large publishing firm. Her mother, an exotic beauty, feminist, and child of Lebanese immigrants, was an author and professor of art at Rutgers University, an avant-garde intellectual.

Ava only made sense of her parents' love after it ended. Opposites may attract, but they rarely grow old together. At first glance, Ava's parents were yin and yang—a levelheaded, rational father and a free-spirited, unpredictable mother. But the nights at home and family vacations included arguments, fights, long awkward silences, and ultimately a sense that everyone was fooling themselves, keeping up a façade until the pair's joint project, Ava, shipped off.

When they announced their intent to divorce shortly before Ava went off to college, she resisted the urge to thank them. She knew the pair would not enjoy a happy or even content marriage with an empty nest.

Growing up, she had all of her material needs more than cared for—they lived in a large house in Maplewood, New Jersey, making day trips to enjoy all of the benefits of pre-Giuliani New York and few of its dangers—but she had been eager to break out of what she found to be stultifying suburbia. The city had taunted her with its proximity, and while her big change-the-world dreams made going to school in Washington tempting, she found herself close to home.

Raj, two years older and from Edison, New Jersey, was another bright mind determined to escape the boring suburbs.

"Look, nobody on the East Coast appreciates people who build things," Raj said as the traffic eked along. "Deep down, you're a builder. An engineer. You build Web sites and systems and networks instead of bricks and mortar, but the basics are the same. Nobody goes to the Ivy League for an engineering degree. It's seen as manual labor."

She laughed. "Glad to see all this dot-com money hasn't eroded that chip on your shoulder," she said.

"Out here, lawyers, bankers, politicians—they're all second-class," he continued. "Nobody here cares much about movie stars or athletes. This is where the nerds get to be in charge and we're the kings of the hill."

"Funny, I used to think of Washington the same way," Ava replied. She tried to remember when she stopped liking D.C.

"Two kinds of kings rule our kingdom," Raj said. "One is the inventor—the one who actually comes up with the idea and makes it happen. The other kind is the venture capitalist. Anybody who can't develop Web-based cold fusion in his garage wants to be the guy who discovered and financed the genius who developed Web-based cold fusion in his garage. It's the star player and manager or coach. Michael Jordan and Phil Jackson."

The traffic moved agonizingly slowly. Pretty heavy for midmorning, thought Ava, frowning.

"Today, when we finally get through this traffic, you're going to meet the next Phil Jackson of Silicon Valley."

. . .

Ava checked in to her hotel in Palo Alto, showered, changed into what she thought were good interview clothes, and Raj drove her to GlobeScape's campus, just a bit off Sand Hill Drive in Menlo Park, at that moment the most expensive patch of commercial real estate in North America.

"Our founder, Len Silver, inherited some wealth from his grandparents' tire company," Raj said.

"Lenny," she chuckled, noticing he looked surprisingly like an old hippie in the company's portrait in the brochure and on the Web site.

"He legally changed it to Lennon in 1980," Raj corrected her. "Invested the wealth he inherited in a few startups, also got in on Apple and Netscape early. I've seen a lot of executives who have brains, but no vision. Well, Lennon Silver has vision by the bucketful."

WIRED PROFILE

When you walk into the Palo Alto offices of GlobeScape .com, the first thing you notice are the giant portraits of world leaders in the hallway leading to the office suite of CEO **Lennon Silver**. They're originals, copying Andy Warhol's Day-Glo-style portraits of Marilyn Monroe: John Kennedy, Gandhi, Che Guevara, Evita Peron. At the end of the hallway is a specially commissioned portrait of Lennon Silver, in the same bold red, green, pink, and blue.

The implicit comparison is a big boast, and Silver is a man determined to back it up.

"I'm not a man who plays it safe," Lennon says in an interview. "I'm different from a lot of other people because I really care about things. I really mean that."

In past years, California investors derided Lennon Silver as one of the higher-risk venture capitalists playing in the silicon sandbox. He racked up some legendary wins—getting in on Apple and Netscape early—and some spectacular failures, including ill-fated efforts to sell produce, jewelry, and coffee beans over the Internet.

Now GlobeScape is Silver's latest thriving baby, and the venture capitalists are swarming. And he's particularly excited about his company's newest project, EasyFed.com. Like many of Silver's ideas, a personal moment of frustration provided the spark of inspiration.

"Some House Budget Subcommittee was talking about increasing the tax rate on carried interest—an absolute war crime of a policy idea—and I had no idea how to get in touch with them," Silver recalls. He found his calls to the IRS, the Joint Tax Committee, and the Securities and Exchange Commission only generated what he called "stunningly unhelpful" responses, and so ending that frustration, on a global scale, became his all-consuming vision.

Enter EasyFed.com, where the average John Q. Public can log on, search for the government service or interaction they require, enter some data and use some drop-down menus, and voilà!—the frustration of taking on City Hall is gone in a puff of electrons.

Silver and his team are betting there's a mint to be made in handling inquiries to the U.S. Mint, but he's playing his cards close to the vest about how EasyFed.com will operate beyond its currently undisclosed—but reportedly quite considerable—sum of venture capital.

Asked to detail EasyFed's revenue model, he demurs. "To truly find something, first you have to lose yourself," he says with a cryptic smile. "Because the Internet is just beginning to reveal its potential."

Ava's first hour on the small GlobeScape campus was a succession of handshakes. Ava kept waiting for some sort of formal interview process, but mostly this was meetings and greetings.

She met plenty of folks whose body language and office location *seemed* important—their titles were "director of inspiration" and "director of innovation," nothing as mundane as a "chief financial officer"—but their questions about her work at the agency seemed perfunctory. Either all that these guys needed to hear was Raj's endorsement, or they simply had faith that she would take to the environment like a fish to water.

The computers on every desk were sleek and astonishingly fast. She knew the equipment back at the agency was dated, but now she felt embarrassed by how clunky and slow her usual tools were.

"The best computers, servers, software, and everything else we could need," Raj beamed.

"This is . . ." She groped for the right word. "*Utopian.*"

"The culture here demands a lot from people, so we need to make sure people have everything they need to do their best work," Raj said.

"That notion is absolutely alien to the federal government," Ava sighed.

Raj chuckled. "It makes a late night—or lots of late nights—a lot easier to deal with when you're enjoying what you're doing. Nobody really worries much about the time clock because what do we love to do? Think, and imagine, and figure stuff out. So we do that for work for a while and then we do that for fun for a while and a lot of the time one blends into another."

Work-life balance problem: solved! thought Ava. *Eliminate the distinction entirely!*

Finally, she was brought to the office suite for Silver. His secretary indicated he would be ready in a few moments. The television was muted on CNBC; later that year GlobeScape was scheduled to have its initial public offering, trading on the NASDAQ under the stock symbol "GlobS."

At last, the secretary looked up and said, "He's ready for you. If he's not at his desk, look in his meditation garden."

. . .

Ava stepped through the doorway, and found a gorgeous office suite with three enormous flat-screen Sony Trinitron televisions, tuned in to CNBC, CNN, and a soap opera; the sound was down on all three. A computer so advanced Ava had never seen it before sat on his desk; a computer she thought had just arrived on the market was half-disassembled in the corner, apparently being put back into its boxes for use elsewhere.

The rear wall's floor-to-ceiling office windows slid open into a large, elaborate, walled garden that stretched around the corner of the building. Ava peered outside, and her eyes readjusted to the bright afternoon sunlight, spying a Buddha statue sitting in a shady corner. Not far away a small fountain bubbled, and orange-and-white carp swam in the waters of a small man-made pond. Over in the farthest corner, on a small wooden platform, the founder sat, meditating.

Lennon Silver was tall, balding, and had a neatly trimmed, graying beard. The remaining hair in the back was tied in a small braid with some sort of shiny metal clip holding it together. He was clad in a polo shirt and khakis, and a pair of glasses lay folded beside him.

"Ava Summers . . ." Silver called out in the garden.

Ava stepped out, a bit bewildered but enjoying the ride. She waited for Silver to speak, but he sat, eyes closed, seemingly deep in meditative peace. She wondered if she was supposed to say something, or whether she would be interrupting. *But he did call me out here*, she thought.

"This is a breathtaking garden," she said.

His eyes opened, and he focused his gaze on her.

"What do you want out of life, Ava?" Silver asked.

It was the strangest interview question she had ever heard, but a pretty good one, she realized. She went with her gut answer.

"To change the world," she answered, a bit ashamed at how far she remained from achieving that lofty goal.

"That's good," he said, his visage breaking into a smile as he rose to his bare feet. "That's my goal, too."

He put on his glasses, strode toward her, extended a hand, and as she took it he kissed her on both cheeks—nothing sexual or aggressive, just a bit more forward than she expected.

"Money doesn't motivate me," he said, unprompted.

"Few rich men *are* motivated by it," Ava said. "Because they've already got it."

Her answer seemed to surprise him, and for a moment he just looked at her, assessing her.

"Walk with me." He strode down the path, and Ava saw the garden was much larger than she thought, curling around the building's corner, vine-covered walls artfully hidden by trees and sculptures.

"We don't build computers anymore. We figure out new things that computers can do," he explained. "I hear you're working small miracles over in the Beltway, using a Commodore 64 and some string."

"Small miracles are all I can make with what I've got back there," she shrugged, relieved that somebody seemed to know her work, as everyone else at the company seemed to regard her background, education, and experience with blithe indifference. "Walking through your offices, this place looks like Starfleet. Or maybe I'm Alice in Wonderland."

"Clarke's third law: Any sufficiently advanced technology is indistinguishable from magic," Silver said with some pride.[24] "I like to think that what we do here, utilizing computers and the Internet in new ways, is really . . . a revolution. I need revolutionaries."

She nodded, smelling some nectarine trees, and realizing that the only things she smelled on the way to the Department of Agriculture most days were car exhaust and the Beltway region's insufferable pollen. "I've been on the establishment side

24 Science fiction author Arthur C. Clarke.

of things for a little too long, I think," she said. "I'm ready to kick-start some revolutions."

"So, you're familiar with Veblen and Romer?"

Ava shook her head. "Was I supposed to meet them before this?"

"Thorstein Veblen was an economist in the late 1800s who predicted engineers would someday run the economy, because the economy moved on technology, and they were the only ones who understood it," Silver said, not looking at her. "He was right, as we all know. The other key visionary economist who shaped me—he's still around—is Paul Romer. He says the economy is like a kitchen. Lots of people can cook, but only a few can take familiar ingredients and create something really new and incredible. Those dishes are wealth. Any society that wants to grow richer will encourage this, and these people are almost entirely nonconformists. Like me and everyone else here."

God, no wonder I can't stand working for the government! thought Ava.

Silver's thoughts seemed to jump around in a way that amused Ava. "They call me founder, they call me CEO, but I really prefer the term 'chief vision officer.' I'm really a force of change—and that's what I'm looking for in the staff around me—not beneath me, but around me. We're a team. A network. Interconnected, not hierarchical."

In her gut, Ava knew she was sold.

. . .

The next day, Ava received an e-mail from GlobeScape's HR department, an offer that struck her as ludicrously generous, with an extraordinarily heavy dollop of stock options as part of the package. Ava responded that she felt very good about the offer, but wanted to take a day or two to think about it. Mostly she wanted to assess the logistics of moving and how quickly she could start. They responded to that message with a second offer that added another five thousand shares in stock options in the third year.

Everything about GlobeScape seemed a little too perfect so far. She kept waiting for the catch. Her father the engineer would have looked at all this and concluded that something wasn't adding up, that there was some hidden factor that explained how the place could seem so ideal . . .

That evening, she dined with Raj.

"So what do you not like about where you work?"

Raj suddenly stopped making eye contact.

"I can't think of anything in particular right now," he said.

"Take your time," she said, not wanting to let him off the hook that easily. She rested her face in her hands. She knew, instantly, that there was something about the place that Raj was hesitant to discuss. *The whole place is a front for the mob*, she guessed to herself. *I'm in a dot-com version of a John Grisham novel.*

"It can be a high-pressure environment," he finally said, looking out the window, past her, at his plate, anywhere but at Ava. "We face very tough competition, a rapidly changing market, the IPO is coming up, and the stakes are very high. There is . . ." He looked for the right word. "Stress." Finally his eyes refocused. "It would be insane to not take this job because of that, though."

"I'm very tempted," Ava said. "I'm probably going to do it, I love the place, it's just . . . it's a big change. Kinda scary."

"Ava, this job could very well be your ticket to spending your life doing whatever you want to do," Raj said.

She couldn't suppress the roll of her eyes.

"That's your Washington cynicism showing," Raj continued. "An engineer who joined Netscape in July 1995 was worth ten million dollars by November. Eighteen months after founding, employees were millionaires."

Ava had never worried that much about money; her parents had made good livings, NYU had been generous with scholarships, and at the Agency of Invasive Species, the pay was okay, nothing special, but the benefits were good. The offer from GlobeScape was huge. But Raj was talking about becoming independently wealthy in a very short period—and he had a particularly excited wide-eyed expression when he talked about this.

"In Silicon Valley, where you work is an enormous gamble. If you work for the right dot-com, within, like, three years you'll have made enough money through stock options to do whatever you want in life for the rest of your life. If you pick the wrong one . . . the venture capitalists might pull the plug one day and you get two weeks' severance. So there's risk. But if you win . . . well, Ava, GlobeScape isn't talking about ideas that will make millions. We think about ideas that will generate *billions*. To start."

Ava nodded, more to herself than to Raj. "The benefit I'm looking forward to the most is going to work each day with enthusiasm."

. . .

Ava couldn't wait to tell her friends about her abrupt career change. She asked Lisa and Jamie to get together after work, at Café Citron, a Latin-fusion place near her apartment.

But the pair reacted with . . . less than full enthusiasm, and after the second "Are you sure?" Ava unleashed a long-repressed torrent of frustration.

"Look, I realized that if I don't get out of that place soon, I'm going to die there, and I don't want you two to die there, either!" Ava said to the recoiling faces of Jamie and Lisa.

"Look, Ava, good for you that you've got this great offer, but just because you hate your job doesn't mean you have to trash ours!" Lisa glared.

"Don't you think that's a little harsh? Nobody dies because they're working at the agency," added Jamie.

"I don't mean you'll physically die there, just your souls," Ava said insistently.

"Oh, *just* that!" shot Jamie.

"Jamie, every week we get together and you say that you feel like you're Humphrey's travel agent! Do you realize that it hurts us to see you so frustrated with your work? You were supposed to be halfway to becoming an international diplomat by now. Are you any closer to putting on the next Yalta Summit?"

"Malta," said Jamie, sighing.

"And you," Ava turned to Lisa. "You feel like you're any closer to becoming White House press secretary?"

Lisa was indignant. "I've had two promotions, and my boss is a few years away from retirement—"

"Oooh, and then you can have his job! Are you really going to be happy writing press releases nobody reads?"

"I can manage my own career, thank you," Lisa fumed.

"Look, if I didn't care about you guys, I wouldn't want you to leave. I woke up! I realized I was wasting my time here, and I think you guys are, too!" Ava said with an anger that surprised her. "We've all been conned. Nobody here wants new blood or new ideas or fresh perspectives. Everyone here wants to do the same damn thing they did the day before, and the same thing tomorrow, and the next day, until they retire. They're just punching a clock. People like us don't belong here, and we never did!"

Jamie looked down at her plate. She knew she had feelings similar to Ava's, but Jamie wondered why Ava felt the need to punctuate a celebratory after-work get-together with ugly truths and deep frustrations.

But Lisa would have none of it. "Oh, there goes poor Ava, she's just so *special*," she sneered. "She's got this million-dollar gee-whiz idea that everybody in the whole agency should listen to, and if they won't let her have her way, then her *special* little mind and *special* little idea will go out to California where all the geniuses out there will listen to her . . ."

The mockery cut Ava to the bone.

"You bitter bitch," she whispered in outrage.

Jamie tried to be the bridge-builder.

"You know, Ava, it's easy for you to say we should just find another job," she began. "You just had this great opportunity fall in your lap. We don't have that."

Ava reached into her purse, grabbed some bills, and threw them on the table, storming out.

From middle school to the Agency of Invasive Species Office of Communications, Lisa Bloom had always taken pride in her work. It was almost a given in Washington; the standard greeting when meeting someone at a party was "So, what do you *do*?" They didn't mean hobbies or interests or what you found most fulfilling; your job title and organization were your identity. Lisa believed Ava hadn't merely contended her job was meaningless but implied *she* was meaningless.

Of course, over the years Lisa shared many job frustrations with Ava, and in fact would, under the influence of sodium pentothal, admit that Ava's warnings of a stagnant, unfulfilling career resonated. That made Ava's rant across the bar table seem like a betrayal; her own doubts and fears, expressed in confidence and often after at least one glass of wine, were thrown back at her to suggest she had made a serious error early in her career, an error compounded each passing day.

Ava departed upon her long cross-country drive without a real goodbye to Lisa; the departure was marked with terse e-mails of "Good luck" and "Thanks."

MARCH 1999

Once settled into the EasyFed team at GlobeScape, Ava worked with two other Web designers and debuggers, the cheery but soft-spoken Willow and the sarcastic Drew, who dressed in black every day except St. Patrick's Day.

"Inspired by Johnny Cash or Richard Lewis?" guessed Ava.

"Richard Belzer," Drew grumbled, not looking up from his screen.

Drew stood out only by the color of his plain T-shirts; much of the GlobeScape staff wore T-shirts, cargo shorts, and flip-flops in the office. Enacting a "casual Friday" policy would have required nudity.

The rare exceptions were when Raj appeared in an impeccable suit.

"The only time most people here dress up is when the Wall Street guys come to town," Raj explained when he stopped by Ava's cubicle. "Three years ago, we had to go to Wall Street for the investors. Now they come to us. Now we decide if we'll let them give us money," he laughed. "The last year has just been crazy. The VCs are just throwing money at us these days."

Behind them, a Vietnamese immigrant paused, then resumed typing.

Ava had been perusing the company pamphlets and wondered who had the kind of money to put into something so vague. "If this business report were any more abstract, it wouldn't have any nouns."

Raj shook his head. "You just don't get it. This could be as big as Microsoft, and bigger, too."

"Pitch me," she dared. "Pretend I'm a potential investor."

He shook his head. "Potential investors aren't as skeptical as you."

"Somehow that's not reassuring," she teased, waving the investor packet. "There's almost nothing in here that gives any indication of how GlobeScape will make those billions you keep talking about."

"Our future earnings will look nothing like our present. Thus, you cannot determine our future value by looking at our present condition,"[25] Raj said, with a bit of indignation.

"We will generate earnings by willing them into spontaneous existence," cracked Drew from his adjacent cubicle.

Raj rolled his eyes. "The old way was generate profits, then attract investors. In the new era, we bring in the investors and that's what fuels the profits."

"Well, I can't wait," Ava chuckled. Finding housing had been harder than she expected, and finding rent at an acceptable apartment took a big bite out of her seemingly massive paycheck.

Still, she found the culture of GlobeScape and the EasyFed team welcoming: Wear what you want, set your own hours, just keep up with your workload. The workload—designing and building the site, testing it. debugging it, testing it again, and so on—was considerable, but Ava felt much more a part of a team than she ever felt at the agency.

"Considering how little time any of us spend at home, our landlords really ought to give us a break," she quipped.

---

25 This is the summary of the investing mind-set of the time offered by Michael Lewis in *The New New Thing: A Silicon Valley Story* (New York: W.W. Norton & Company, 2001).

"Why go home? What's there?" chuckled Willow from the next cubicle.

Ava sent a quick "HOW ARE YOU DOING?" e-mail to Jamie and Lisa.

Jamie offered a lengthy e-mail about her wedding planning; Lisa responded merely, "Fine. Busy."

JUNE 1999

"Marketing just unveiled our logo," Drew announced.

All of their Netscape browsers visited the same site simultaneously. A bizarre, beaked, pinkish-purple one-eyed squid stared back at them.

"What the hell is that thing?" exclaimed Ava in horror.

"Squiggy the Squicken?!" Willow read aloud.

"It's like H. P. Lovecraft's Happy Meal toy," Drew said.

The Birth of Squiggy

Focus group data indicated that when consumers think of the "federal government" or "federal bureaucracy," the animal that most often comes to mind is "octopus." This is a choice with heavy historical symbolism, as the image of the animal reaching out and squeezing things with long tentacles has been used in cartoons, posters, and other political art, referring to Big Oil or Big Business, Nazis, Jews, Communists, etc. The image is always alien, unfamiliar, menacing, sinister, powerful; its actions are often hidden or hard to see.

When asked for the animal with the opposite qualities—nonthreatening, amusing, common, harmless—the animal that was mentioned most often was "chicken."

As EasyFed is designed to make dealing with the federal

government easier, we decided to take the image associated with negative perceptions of the federal government and give it the appealing, funny, harmless qualities associated with the opposite: Thus, the Squicken. Friendly, fun, and cuddly.

"It's like the sushi from hell," Ava lamented to Raj.

Ava and Raj weren't a couple, per se. They hadn't been dating, nor had their increasingly close friendship ever been interrupted by negotiations on the terms of exclusivity. But on a regular basis, she and he would get together at one of their places, order delivery food, and watch movies or just drink bottles of wine and talk into the night. Sometimes they had sex, sometimes they didn't; sometimes they slept over, sometimes they didn't. Periodically Ava found herself wanting something more solid with him, but her nagging doubts persisted. Raj periodically would comment that his parents were urging him to get married, and that his having rejected an arranged marriage, they expected him to bring home a nice Indian girl.

And in perhaps the clearest warning sign of his flaws as a serious mate, Raj was an enthusiastic fan of Squiggy, the one-eyed mutant corporate logo that started to appear in Ava's dreams.

"Squiggy is going to be *huge*," Raj promised. "Pets.com was going to make money off pet supply stuff, but one of their biggest sellers is the sock puppet!"

Worse, Raj bailed at the last second as Ava's date to Jamie's wedding.

JULY 1999

Ava flew cross-country to Florida, where Jamie was marrying her Marine boyfriend; soon she would be Jamie Caro-Marcus; Ava joked that said quickly, her name sounded Greek.

Ava and Lisa ended up sitting at the same table. Ava wondered if Jamie's wedding seating chart secretly intended to force some détente or reconciliation between the two women, but it merely reflected that her parents had obliviously lumped the brides' "Washington friends" together at one table.

Lisa and Ava finally did find each other in a hallway off the hotel ballroom . . . after several glasses of wine and two champagne toasts.

"I'm really sorry the way we left things," Ava began.

Lisa relaxed a bit. "I'm really glad you said that," she said, "because I wanted to be happy for you going out to California, and after what you said, I couldn't. I felt like you were laughing at us."

"I would never do that!" Ava said. "I love you guys! We've been through so much crap together!"

"Ladies, use your inside voices!" said one of the older guests.

"I know!" Lisa said, ignoring the complaint. "And I want you to find your dream job!"

"Thank you! I think this is my dream job—I mean, if the launch goes right. Otherwise, it's my nightmare job."

They embraced, until a couple of the groom's buddies started hooting and hollering.

"So, what's new at the agency?"

Lisa thought for a moment. "Um . . ." She paused, then sighed. "Nothing, really." The girls laughed.

Lisa attributed her assessment to the amount of alcohol she had enjoyed so far—but she had a nagging sense that if sober, she would have still been groping for anything that qualified as new, or different, or interesting enough to share.

AUGUST 1999

EasyFed's launch date loomed, less than a week away.

The Saturday evening before it, GlobeScape rented a 53-room mansion in Burlingame, California, for the launch party.

The two hundred GlobeScape employees working on the EasyFed project, another hundred spouses and dates, and easily three hundred guests crammed into the mansion and its grounds. The group ran out of the complimentary fleece jackets with the EasyFed logo. "Swag bags" of key chains, mouse pads, and other tchotchkes with the EasyFed logo were distributed as well. Tuxedo-clad waiters brought around silver platters of hors d'oeuvres and canapés, and the line at the open bar was long.

"This is . . . so ostentatious," Ava gasped. "Even Gatsby would tell us to tone it down a little."

"It's all about generating buzz," Willow said with a giggle. "Everybody's going to be writing about us—*Red Herring, Business 2.0, Salon, Slate.*"

Even Drew had loosened up. "This is totally going to show those hotshots at Pseudo.com."

The mansion's tennis courts were functioning as a helipad for the evening. Silver's helicopter, sleek and the color of his surname, landed, giving the executive an entrance most Hollywood action heroes would envy. He strode to the assembled partygoers like a conquering hero, reveling in their already-inebriated cheers for a few moments before beginning some remarks.

"My friends, this evening we celebrate a dawn!" Silver roared, as the partygoers applauded a thoroughly dysfunctional metaphor. "We stand on the precipice of a new age. We are not merely some dot-com dreamers; we are revolutionaries!" More cheers.

Silver spoke from the edge of a large, padded platform.

A row of about a dozen men in red ninja-like costumes marched in a line behind him, each holding a rolled-up piece of scarlet cloth.

"What's with the Mortal Kombat guys?" Ava asked.

"Silver brought in some Chinese dance troupe to perform— 'Tie My Wee' or something," Drew cracked.

Willow had found a program for the evening. "The Qing Yi Yin Xiang Shen Ke Dai Zi," she read aloud. "They're supposed to be some big performers over in Shanghai, doing a West Coast tour. They perform the 'Dance of the Crimson Banner.'"

Then the crowd laughed, because Silver had said something he thought was funny, and most of the partygoers were drunk.

Silver concluded, "You've all done a lot of work to get to this point, and our revolution has already begun!" He turned to the short, limber men behind him and nodded.

As one, the dancers unfurled small red flags in each hand and began to spin. The dancers probably cost a fortune, but they did know how to put on a show. Their act accelerated as it went on, as each performer began demonstrating spectacular leaps, flips, cartwheels, and other acrobatics. Their crimson banners snapped and fluttered dramatically with each move, and they departed by backflipping and cartwheeling through the crowded audience on their way to their vans, to roaring, drunken cheers.

Ava, Willow, Drew, and Raj drank until the booze ran out,

and then waited for the small fleet of taxicabs that GlobeScape had called in advance.

It was only on the way out, stuck in a traffic jam upon the driveway, that Ava realized that EasyFed had celebrated its debut with a parade of waving red flags.

8

AUGUST 1999
U.S. National Debt: $5.6 trillion
Budget, USDA Bureau of Invasive Species: $162.33 million

E asyFed.com was scheduled to launch at 6:00 a.m. Eastern time—3:00 a.m. local—on Wednesday, September 1. When the hour arrived, the UNDER CONSTRUCTION sign was gone . . . and a blank screen greeted visitors. For about one hour, absolute pandemonium reigned in the Palo Alto headquarters, as some unforeseen technical glitch delayed the much-touted debut. Thanks in no small part to Ava, the bug was identified and corrected and the site went live, a mere two hours late.

OCTOBER 1999

From time to time, Silver liked to bring people into the conference room for what he called 'vision talks'—what he undoubtedly believed were inspirational speeches. Ava, Willow, and Drew found them increasingly hard to follow or bear.

The early traffic numbers had been good but not great—other than the 0 visitors successfully logged in during the initial two hours. But month by month, details of the GlobeScape

IPO became scarcer and scarcer. Finally, around Columbus Day, the company announced that it had been pushed back into 2000, "when the market won't be so crowded with IPOs."

Word in the GlobeScape hallways was that Lennon Silver was particularly cranky lately. When news came that another vision talk was hastily scheduled, the office's temperature seemed to drop ten degrees.

The EasyFed team stood around the conference room with a new pensiveness.

"Money does not motivate me . . ." Silver began. "Revolution does. . . . But our investors need results, they need reassurance about their return on investment. They're proving less patient than I expected—quite reasonably, I would add. So, if I cannot show them ROI, I can show them signs of the revolution advancing."

He looked out on the collected employees, everyone vaguely concerned but not sure what, exactly, constituted a sign of the revolution advancing.

"Are we revolutionaries?" Silver bellowed.

The response was insufficiently enthusiastic.

"I said, 'Are we revolutionaries?' You, are you a revolutionary?" he pointed to Chin-Ho Kyun. He was one of the new hires, a rather intimidated South Korean immigrant. He looked mortified to be called upon in front of everyone, and his eyes bulged in fearful confusion.

"I am . . . a programmer," Kyun stammered.

"That's NOT GOOD ENOUGH!" Silver pounded the conference table. "Clean out your desk!"

"But he's—"

Silver shot the objector a furious look. Kyun lowered his head and quickly exited the room.

He pointed to another terrified employee. "Are you a revolutionary?

This one had learned from Kyun's painful lesson: "YES!"

Ava marveled at what she saw. She exchanged an uncomfortable glance with Willow. Could an employer do this? What was the point of this insane ritual?

Kyun had barely been here a month, and seemed to be doing good work. She realized Silver had no idea who Kyun was, and didn't realize he had just fired one of his better employees. He appeared to be firing people for the sake of firing people, or to motivate the rest of them.

Silver went to the deputy head of marketing. "Are you a revolutionary?"

"Yes," said the unshaven twentysomething, barely able to repress a roll of his eyes.

"I want to hear it in your voice! I want to see it in your eyes! We are about overturning old, established authorities! Show me your revolutionary spirit!"

The deputy head of marketing reached his limit. "Oh, screw this," he said, brushing past Silver and heading to the door. "I've been in talks with Yahoo!, I don't need to take this crap."

Silver's face registered betrayal for a split second, but then he resumed his messianic pose. "Good! Go ahead! I don't need counterrevolutionaries who hedge their bets! I need true believers!"

From a standing position, the surprisingly spry Silver leaped onto the conference table.

"ARE YOU A REVOLUTIONARY?"

"Yes!" the assembled employees shouted, in a mix of enthusiasm and fear that they were witnessing a nervous breakdown.

"I SAID, ARE YOU A REVOLUTIONARY?!"

"YES!"

As she chanted her approval alongside Willow and Drew, Ava realized the predictable boredom of the Agency of Invasive Species had never looked so good.

NOVEMBER 1999

The traffic numbers slid a bit, to the merely mediocre, but not all of the news was bad for EasyFed that autumn; on Thanksgiving, the "Squiggy the Squicken" balloon made its debut in the Macy's Thanksgiving Day Parade, right between Lou Bega and Charlotte Church. While that traffic spike proved short-lived, the marketing department assured everyone that the site's biggest publicity effort would shock and amaze.

JANUARY 2000

A gigantic chunk of the advertising and marketing budget for EasyFed.com—$1.1 million—was spent on the airtime for a thirty-second nationwide ad during the broadcast of Super Bowl XXXIV on January 30.

The ad began by showing a harried Ernest Borgnine at his desk with a computer, his tables strewn with paper, and lamenting, "File my taxes online? Apply for a small business grant through the Internet? I can't understand any of this stuff!" At no point did the ad-makers feel any particular need to explain why the star of *McHale's Navy* and *Airwolf* was applying for a grant from the U.S. Department of Commerce.

A computer-generated Squiggy, about the size of a traffic cone, popped out of Borgnine's coffee cup, and immediately began waving his tentacles toward Borgnine's computer keyboard.

"I can help, Ernie!"

Instead of immediately beating the strange, pinkish-purple, one-eyed beaked cephalopod to death with his shoe, as most people's instincts would dictate, Borgnine exclaimed, "Squiggy the Squicken!" in joyous recognition. Apparently it had taken the actor several takes to get the portmanteau correct, and the director had to keep explaining it wasn't a "Squidge-ken."

"Have government Web sites got you seeing red? Try Easy-Fed!" chirped the unnervingly happy squid, with an eye that the Taiwanese computer animators had depicted with perhaps a bit too much realism. "EasyFed.com helps you get the information you need, and fast! Simple, easy and quick!" as the tentacles typed with blurring speed.

GRANT APPLICATION APPROVED! appeared in giant letters on Borgnine's computer screen in a font no government Web site had ever used. Underneath the actor's beaming face, fine white print clarified, "Results not typical. EasyFed.com is not responsible for the results of any interaction with any agency on its customers' behalf, and government response times vary greatly."

"Thanks, Squiggy!"

"Remember, there's no need to dread! Try EasyFed instead!"

The squid did a cartwheel on its tentacles off the desk and past a window, where an aging Michael McKean and David Lander appeared as their characters from *Laverne & Shirley.* "I remember when I was everyone's favorite Squiggy," lamented Lander.

Across America, roughly eighty-eight million Super Bowl watchers, previously enjoying the St. Louis Rams build a 16–6 lead over the Tennessee Titans, all simultaneously turned to each other and asked, "What the hell was that thing?"

The *USA Today* ad-meter reviewing the commercials the following morning suggested that test audiences and online respondents graded the ad medium-to-bad, suggesting that the audiences liked its protagonists and remembered it, but found it bizarre and were vague on the actual product being sold. But the ad scored off the charts with the advertising professionals, who praised its humor, creativity, and unpredictability.

The ad garnered a lot of mockery from the likes of Dennis Miller, Dave Barry, and James Lileks. George Will declared, "It is long past time for mandatory drug testing of Madison Avenue's creative staff."

But in the following days, traffic at EasyFed.com was up considerably, almost as much as at the Web sites devoted to Ernest Borgnine and *Laverne & Shirley*.

FEBRUARY 2000

Ava was crestfallen. "What do you mean you're leaving?"

Raj broke the news before Kozmo.com had delivered their Ben & Jerry's and the night's direct-to-video cheese-fest starring Marc Singer.

Ava was in no mood to be blindsided by more bad news. Her hours in the office had been lengthening, not shortening. Silver was acting increasingly erratic, and a mood of nervousness and paranoia had descended upon the office like a cloud of poison gas.

Raj explained he would be leaving GlobeScape in two weeks to take some job in Boston. He talked about what a great opportunity it was, but seemed evasive on what this consulting firm did and what precisely he would be doing. What had been unthinkable was that Raj hadn't mentioned anything about any of this before announcing he would be taking the job and moving across the country.

A strange question popped into her mind. "Have your stock options even vested yet?"

He shrugged.

And with that evasion, Ava felt something turn within her. *Good riddance,* she thought, glaring.

MARCH 2000

Rumors of layoffs were louder and more frequent.

Finally, one morning the entire branch was asked, via e-mail, to assemble in the conference room again. This meant a meeting of more people than the room was ever meant to include, and the temperature rose uncomfortably. Silver came in, ten minutes late.

"As you have heard, our seed funders are . . . growing impatient," he said quietly. "With our sites not yet revenue-neutral, we need to demonstrate that we can cut costs until the turnaround accelerates."

He looked around the room, recognizing some people, not recognizing many others.

"I believe in looking people in the eye when we need to let someone go," he said, picking up a sheet of paper he had entered with.

"Chat . . . Chatur . . ."

"Chaturvedi," said a frustrated techie in the back.

"Yup, that's the one."

"Which one? There are three of us here."

"Vivek."

"Vivek P. or Vivek R.?"

Silver looked blankly at the sheet in front of him. "It doesn't say here . . . I'm going to have to check with human resources. We'll come back to that one."

Silver mispronounced one name after another during the long, awkward meeting.

One by one, the names were read off. A few cried. A relative veteran employee burst out with frustration, "This is a bunch of bull, man!"

Silver worked through a dozen names. Then a second dozen.

"I just got my business cards printed!" groaned one of the newer faces.

APRIL 2000

That night, Ava called Jamie—to check in, to vent, to cry a little, and to get a much-needed laugh or two.

Jamie reported that married life had proven joyous so far, and that life at the Agency of Invasive Species continued as it had for most of the preceding years. The appointed director remained virtually invisible, Administrative Director Adam Humphrey continued to manage, Deputy Administrative Director Jack Wilkins put out fires as necessary.

And Jamie admitted she still felt like a travel agent some days, continuing to arrange for Humphrey to travel to far-flung destinations for conferences.

The next night, Lisa called Ava—to announce that she was now the assistant director of communications . . . and to admit that with her new title, she still felt like she distributed information no one cared to read, and ignored or diverted the requests for information that anyone might actually want to read.

JUNE 2000

The next round of layoffs did not include a personal announcement from the CEO. Those being cut were invited to the conference room. The old rule was that if you weren't invited to a meeting, it was bad news because you were out of the loop. The new rule was that if you weren't invited to a meeting, you probably weren't getting laid off today.

But one Thursday, a particularly large group was asked to

attend the meeting. Willow was among them. Drew and Ava were not.

"I'm sorry," Ava said.

"It's just a matter of time for all of us," said Drew, in his way of being reassuring.

Willow departed to get the bad news.

Two guys from the remains of the sales team strolled into the office and looked over Willow's desk. Consulting a printed-out e-mail, one nodded to the other, "Yup, Willow Potts. She was on the list."

The other looked over her desk—still cluttered with the papers and other detritus of work from less than twenty minutes ago—and started removing the staplers, pen holders, and other office supplies.

"What the hell do you think you're doing?" Ava asked angrily.

"It's not like she's going to need it," the younger sales guy shrugged.

"Scavengers!" she gasped.

AUGUST 2000

On Capitol Hill, Congressman Nick Bader was starting to wonder if the entire U.S. government was some elaborate practical joke on him, as each effort to get the power he wanted left him feeling even more powerless to achieve his goals.

He had finally been allowed to join one of his colleagues, Tom Coburn, for a meeting with Senate Majority Leader Trent Lott, a Mississippi pork enthusiast whom Bader had found to be an insufferable disappointment. The pair laid out, in great length and detail, how the latest omnibus appropriations bill, responsible for funding the government, had been a disaster.

Not only was it huge and stuffed to the gills with waste, but Coburn insisted it amounted to a complete repudiation of what Republicans claimed to stand for, and a betrayal of the concept of "good government."

The Senate majority leader was unmoved. "Well, I've got an election coming up in 2000," he said. "After that we can have good government."[26]

Coburn fumed, and Bader had to stifle so much rage that he snapped the pencil he was holding.

Afterward, Bader ran into another one of his budget hawk allies, a newly elected member and budget wonk from his home state.

"How did it go?" asked Pat Toomey. "Does the Senate leadership understand what we're trying to say, or not?"

"Do you remember in *Indiana Jones*, where they're on a plane, and they think everything's fine, and then the plane starts shaking, and they sense things aren't fine, so they go up to the cockpit?" Bader rambled, a little shell-shocked with disappointment. "And then they open the door and gasp, seeing two empty seats and no pilots and a mountain right in front of them?"

Bader sighed, shook his head, and refocused with a wide-eyed, befuddled stare.

"Pat, nobody's flying our plane!"

26 Sen. Tom Coburn, *Breach of Trust*, p. xix.

9

MARCH 2001
U.S. National Debt: $5.7 trillion
Budget, USDA Agency of Invasive Species: $175.93 million

Humphrey and Wilkins departed the Department of Agriculture building, walking along the National Mall to look at a site that the administrative director declared would be the next location of the Agency of Invasive Species Headquarters Building. Wilkins thought his boss was wildly over-optimistic.

Wilkins shook his head with a skeptical laugh. "There's no way the Mall bosses are going to sign off on this."

They stood before an unused triangle of land, where the grass grew thin, bordered by Independence Avenue from the north, Maine Avenue to the west, 15th Street to the east. Maine and 15th intersect at the southernmost point. Directly to the northeast was the Washington Monument.

"I've been suggesting sites to the National Capital Planning Commission for the past eight years now," Humphrey said. "They're more receptive to this than to any of my previous proposals."

"Yeah, because your other ones were even more ridiculous," Wilkins chuckled. "How long did it take them to laugh you out of their office when you proposed a site that would have views of both the Washington Monument *and* the White House? They'd never put something there."

"Actually, word is that they're going to put the National Museum of African American History there."

"Really? There?" Wilkins winced. "I mean, it's good to have one—although I guess I'm wondering why you would want it separate from the National Museum of American History."

"Probably because they'll soon finish the National Native American History Museum, and eventually they'll have to address the proposal for the national Latino Museum," Humphrey shrugged. "It's a land rush, Jack. The Dwight Eisenhower Memorial—"

"Wait, you mean separate from the World War II Memorial?"

"The victims of Ukrainian famine, the United States Air Force Memorial, the Victims of Communism Memorial, the Thomas Masaryk Memorial—"

"I have no idea who that is."

"First president of Czechoslovakia."

"Ooh, I have a good spot for that one! How about Prague, does that work for them?" Wilkins rolled his eyes.

"The American Veterans Disabled for Life Memorial. They're jamming the Japanese-American Internment Camps memorial on a narrow little traffic triangle by Union Station.[27] In the future, everyone will have a memorial or monument for fifteen minutes."

"To be carved in stone at the Andy Warhol Memorial," Wilkins griped. "Good luck getting the funding for all these, particularly with a Republican in the White House."

"That's the thing, Jack," Humphrey said with a smile. "You

---

27 All of the proposals Humphrey mentions are actual completed memorials and museums in downtown Washington, in-progress works, or proposals before the National Capital Planning Commission.

notice we haven't needed our traditional battle-stations meetings, no dire sense of a budgetary threat from a new Republican coming to Washington, no sudden embrace of the latest Bader plan to cut us to the bone." He nodded in the direction of the White House. "This one doesn't have any of that budgetary ferocity. His enthusiasm for faith-based government services, his repeated emphasis that he's a . . ." Humphrey momentarily squinted his eyes and held his hands to his heart, "*compassionate* conservative, the belief that government should help people . . . George W. Bush did not come to Washington to cut spending."

"You realize you're saying this with Republicans controlling the House, and the Senate, depending on what side of the bed Jim Jeffords woke up on this morning." Wilkins laughed a bit at the irony. "So after all these years, these ninnies have finally made peace with government spending?"

. . .

Ava expected the layoff notice from EasyFed to trigger another round of heartbreak, but she found it liberating.

The EasyFed site had more and more portions that said, "This page is currently undergoing maintenance." Updates grew more infrequent, and traffic dwindled. Some pages failed to load entirely and dead links multiplied. Like a dying relative, Ava wanted to see someone pull the plug and end the suffering. She joked that some sites should come with prearranged DNRs—"Do Not Reload."

She expected the decline of the site to generate humiliating criticism and mockery, but she realized that everyone who would write about it in the dot-com world was undergoing the same ritual sacrifice of mass layoffs. It was brutal out there.

It was brutal inside, too. Ava outlasted Drew—he said

farewell by setting fire to a pile of long-awaited business cards on the sidewalk outside GlobeScape headquarters—and she found that she knew only a small fraction of her remaining coworkers. Those that remained seemed to keep their heads down and rarely said hello in the hallways. The GlobeScape offices grew emptier, and the EasyFed team kept getting moved to smaller and more cramped spaces—the cubicle farms went from free range to a setup that the ASPCA would find intolerably cruel for livestock. She introduced herself to new officemates, "Hi, I'm Ava Summers, and I'm the Angel of Dot-Com Death. Within a few months we'll be moving offices again, and half of our coworkers won't be here."

When GlobeScape announced that the EasyFed project was going "on hiatus," she knew it was dead.

The good news was that with her failure to use any vacation days or sick days, and the fact that GlobeScape as a whole continued to operate, Ava departed the building with about three months' worth of severance and unused paid vacation.

Freed from the monotony of staring at a computer monitor for a thoroughly unhealthy majority of her waking hours, Ava finally started enjoying living out on the West Coast.

It was on a park bench in San Diego, looking out at the U.S.S. *Midway*, that she sensed she just had to chalk up her tumultuous roller coaster ride of EasyFed as an adventure she had to take, just to determine finally that she in fact *didn't* belong out here. She didn't quite miss her old life at the Agency of Invasive Species, but she found she missed Washington.

Californians were relaxed, easygoing, and fun, but . . . too relaxed, she found. Sure, half the time you would walk through Palo Alto and bump into people obsessing with their cellular phones, but she realized that most of the tech-heads out here were missing part of the equation. They obsessed over what their gadgets could do—and often how lucrative they could be—but rarely if ever talked about how they affected the world that used them. Something about the language of her industry—seeing people as consumers and market share—left Ava cold. They were people, and she remembered coming out of NYU with a fire in her eyes to use technology to change the world—and not just in unveiling a faster Web browser that would be overtaken by the competition within six months.

She stood up from the bench and resolved: She would return to Washington . . . as soon as she could find a decent-sounding job back there.

AUGUST 2001

"Condit's been somebody we could count on," sighed Wilkins as the morning news replayed the previous night's catastrophically awful interview between the congressman and Connie Chung. Wilkins rubbed his head, turned off the small television in Humphrey's office, and wandered toward the couch, wondering why Humphrey seemed so unperturbed about the nationally televised PR self-immolation of one of their better allies on Capitol Hill. "Why's he doing this?" Wilkins asked Humphrey, seated at the desk and focused upon a stack of paperwork. "Can't he see he's making himself radioactive?"

"Why's he doing what, precisely?" Humphrey asked, looking up with one cocked eyebrow, attempting to stifle a mischievous and largely inappropriate grin.

"Well, for starters, being dumb enough to bang an intern!" exclaimed Wilkins, falling to the couch.

Humphrey's smirk now reached the status of an elite running back; he couldn't stop it but could only hope to contain it. "Two years ago, didn't we have almost precisely the same conversation?"

Wilkins rolled his eyes. "This is different!"

"Indeed," Humphrey clucked. "As far as we know, Congressman Condit has never testified under oath about that poor girl. It is also different in that President Clinton knew that his position within his party made his resignation unacceptable to hundreds of powerful people. If he had stepped down, and Al Gore had become president, little or nothing would have changed in terms of policies—in fact, he probably would have won last year as a quasi-incumbent presiding over peace and prosperity. But enough powerful people had worked and struggled and sweated to put Bill Clinton in that office, and they weren't about to see him depart over something they deemed as . . . insufficiently consequential as . . . 'banging an intern,' as you so eloquently put it."

Wilkins shook his head. "Monica Lewinsky never went missing!"

"True," shrugged Humphrey. "But what Congressman Condit is attempting is the same wait-it-out maneuver as Clinton. I use that strategy regularly—hunker down, delay in every way possible, and wait for your opponents and critics to become distracted. I like to think of it as one of the useful potions in my studies of bureaucratic alchemy, and I wish I could have trademarked it. Clinton at least used it well. But with Condit, today it's . . . well, it's maddening to watch a perfectly respectable and well-regarded tactic used so *amateurishly*."

. . .

Ava's return preceded the discovery of that decent-sounding job; the tech bust that had left a deep chill of hiring freezes over Silicon Valley had struck most nongovernmental entities in the nation's capital as well.

Ava found a nice one-bedroom a bit south of Dupont Circle—a seemingly near-ideal neighborhood suddenly in the national spotlight for the most macabre of reasons: some congressional intern who lived across the street had disappeared and become a bizarre, tawdry media obsession.

But she relished having Jamie and Lisa over for cheap red wine and a reconnection.

"I'm on New Hampshire Avenue now," Ava said. "When you hit the TV trucks, you've gone too far."

SEPTEMBER 2001

The federal offices opened up again. The National Guard Humvees started packing up.

There was an effort to get back to "normal," but a lot of folks watched televisions that had been put in for keeping up on events or emergency information. No one really objected or claimed they were a distraction. The new, ominous news tickers ran across the bottom of the screen, little constantly flowing rivers of anxiety in all-caps Helvetica Narrow font.

Wilkins found himself sitting on the couch in Humphrey's office.

"I'm thinking of scrapping it all and enlisting," Wilkins said. "I know they don't need any more forty-five-year-old career civil service employees, but maybe they need somebody to . . . I don't know, fill out forms somewhere, to free up somebody else who can go and do something useful and find these—"

"Jack," Humphrey interrupted. "As we speak, our very finest are arming themselves and preparing to bring justice, in its most lethal forms, to our enemies," Humphrey said. "By the time any branch of the armed services figures out what to do with you, the fight will be over. We should, however, think of how we can assist in the protection of our nation, in our own humble way."

The momentary heart-to-heart over, Humphrey rose to his feet and purposely strode back toward the desk. "I ask you: What is the one form of aviation that this agency deals with all the time and enjoys virtually unparalleled expertise?"

"Caro says you fly to conferences more often than—"

"Er, no, not commercial flight. Crop dusters, Jack!" the formality returned. "Look at this!"

> On September 23, 2001, at the request of Attorney General John Ashcroft, the government grounded all the crop dusters in America—over five thousand planes that ordinarily spray pesticides on crops.
>
> James Lester, an airplane maintenance worker in Belle Glade, Florida, identified Atta from photographs shown him by the FBI after the September 11th attack. He said he was one of a group of 12–15 "arab-looking" men who had visited the airport and asked about crop dusters, including the weekend of September 9–10, 2001.[28]

"And this!" Humphrey handed over a transcript of a presidential news conference:

> **Reporter:** You talk about the general threat toward Americans. You know, the Internet is crowded with all sorts of rumor and gossip and, kind of, urban myths. And people ask, what is it they're supposed to be on the lookout for? Other than the twenty-two most wanted

28 Edward Jay Epstein, http://www.edwardjayepstein.com/nether_fictoid11.htm. "But the hijackers had left Florida prior to that weekend and the FBI had charge-card receipts and car-rental records that put Atta in New York and Boston on the weekend of September 9-10th. If so, Atta could not have been part of the group of 'Arab-looking' men that visited the Belle Glade Airport that weekend."

terrorists, what are Americans supposed to look for and report to the police or to the FBI?

President Bush: Well, Ann, you know, if you find a person that you've never seen before getting in a crop duster that doesn't belong to you—report it.

"What are you thinking?" Wilkins asked when he was finished reading.

"Jack," Humphrey said proudly, "our country needs us. It's time to show how we can help our country. Hargis can make this happen."

. . .

A few days later, Humphrey and Wilkins were wanded repeatedly by the U.S. Capitol Police as they headed into Rayburn House Office Building.

Hargis was aging but no less beloved by the voters in Kentucky's Seventh Congressional District.

"I cannot believe that old coot!" Vernon Hargis fumed with a phlegmy gurgle. "Two days after the attacks—we could have lost this building!—Byrd is getting two million dollars for a new computer network at the 'Robert C. Byrd Regional Training Institute' at the Army National Guard's Camp Dawson in West Virginia. Now he's talking about turning the whole place into a National Counterterrorism Training Center!"

"Yikes," exclaimed Wilkins. "Pretty crass to start sniffing around for pork at a time like this."

"Crass?" grumbled Hargis. "I'm mostly pissed I didn't think of it first!"

Humphrey cleared his throat.

"Congressman, I'd like to turn your attention to another facet of the terrorist threat that our agency may be able to contribute to . . ." he began as he reached into his briefcase. "You're familiar with the discussion of terrorists spreading chemical or biological weapons through the use of *crop dusters*."

"Damn if I'm not having nightmares about it!" bellowed the congressman. "You look up, see some small plane, and then POOF—some toxic crap is making your hair fall out and you break into boils. Makes a man nostalgic for the simplicity of the old-fashioned mushroom cloud."

"Indeed, Congressman, a threat like no other. What you may not know is that perhaps no other federal agency deals with crop dusters more than ours . . ."

"What about the Federal Aviation—eh, yeah. I see," the congressman said.

"They've got a lot on their minds right now," Wilkins said.

"Which pesticides and chemicals could be most harmful to human health, dispersal patterns, which types of crop dusters can do what—Congressman, this is our bread and butter. Let us help our nation during this darkest of hours by converting one of our facilities in your district into . . . the Agency of Invasive Species' National Center for Crop Duster Security."

Hargis didn't say anything for a few moments, which was not like him.

"Maybe . . ." he said quietly. "Byrd's already getting grief for what he's doing with Camp Dawson. I'm going to need paperwork—some compelling stuff to show that this is worthwhile . . . How serious is this threat?"

"Florida crop dusters discussing their meetings with Mohammed Atta is insufficiently serious?" Humphrey exclaimed with a bit of indignation. "Congressman, you tell whoever needs to hear it that our familiarity with the mechanics of this activity and . . . the information available to us points to a serious and persistent al-Qaeda threat to American agriculture."

Hargis's eyes bulged. Wilkins wondered if Humphrey knew what he was implying.

"You've heard about something?" gasped the congressman. "Your pilots or pesticide dealers on the ground met with other terrorists or something?"

Humphrey played his hand carefully. "Congressman, at this point, I would be remiss if I ruled anything in or out. As you know, many Americans are reevaluating past interactions with slightly suspiciously behaving young Arab men."

"Apparently the moment Mohammed Atta's mug shot hit the airwaves, the FBI got thousands of calls from people claiming to have talked to him," Wilkins added.

"Mundane interactions and unusual questions now take on a much more sinister light. Like everyone else, we're trying to sort out fact from rumor. Our particular specialty, species that come in and wreak ecological havoc with crops and water supplies and such, well . . . it makes a chill go down one's spine, the thought of the evil men of al-Qaeda focusing their energies in that direction. But . . . in light of the consequences, I don't think we can dismiss any possibility, now can we?"

Hargis nodded. "Humph . . . I'll use my utmost discretion."

The Washington Post

Fears Ground Crop-Dusting Flights Again

WASHINGTON—FBI and Federal Aviation Administration officials banned crop-dusting flights Sunday amid new reports that terrorists sought the use of the planes in launching a biological or chemical attack.

Lawmakers are said to be particularly concerned about intelligence reports from the Department of Agriculture's Agency of

Invasive Species, indicating that al-Qaeda may be looking beyond ordinary bioweapons and poisons to attempts to import
invasive species to wreak havoc upon U.S. cropland and water
supplies.

Wilkins greeted Humphrey with a copy of the *Post* at the Department of Agriculture's front door.

"Hargis blabbed!" he screamed.

Humphrey shushed him, and pulled him aside in the building's hallway. "Yes, Jack, he's a congressman, that's what he
does."

"What are we going to do?"

"Nothing. This can only help our effort to create a National
Center for Crop Duster Security."

"He thinks we know that al-Qaeda is trying to smuggle invasive species into the country!"

"He misinterpreted my remarks," Humphrey shrugged.
"Despite our best efforts, miscommunications occur all the
time. I can only be responsible for what I say, not the conclusions he draws from the information we provided."

"You knew how he would react! You were deliberately
ambiguous!"

"Strategic ambiguity has been good enough for our China
policy for years, I don't see why it would be a problem here and
now," Humphrey said.

The two strode until they reached the lobby outside Hum-
phrey's office, where the administrative director's secretary,
Carla, appeared to be trying to placate a Eurasian Wonder
Woman in a perfectly tailored business suit.

"Mr. Humphrey, this woman is from . . . *somewhere* and she
insists upon speaking to you immediately," Carla announced.

The Woman from Somewhere was about 5′5″, wore fairly
high stiletto heels and a professional but snug business suit. She

had long dark hair and glasses. Wilkins was reminded of the female Secret Service agents he had seen, but this woman was indisputably striking—and more than a little intimidating.

"I'm sorry, Ms. . . ."

"Just call me Karina, Mr. Humphrey," the woman declared with a ferocity barely chained behind sufficient formality.

"Karina . . ." Humphrey waited for a last name.

"That's all you need to know," she said curtly. "Your recent statements to lawmakers about information indicating 'a serious and persistent al-Qaeda threat to American agriculture' have raised some eyebrows among your fellow government employees in *Langley*. If you've heard something we haven't, we would very much like you to share. If, as I suspect, you're just hyping a nonexistent threat to grab a bit of the funding pie, cease and desist immediately. Those of us fighting a real battle don't need to have our mission complicated by opportunists."

She glanced at Wilkins, and he promptly succumbed to dry mouth and squeaked a hello.

"The same lawmakers that you try to con a budget out of also think they should tell my bosses what to do," she continued, eyes flashing with fury. "So if you guys tell them that al-Qaeda's about to launch an attack of Pod People, I will get panicking ninnies on Hipsy and Sipsy[29] telling my bosses to get somebody on Pod People–watch immediately. And I don't want to say I couldn't stop the next attack because some idiot thought it would be a good idea to put me and my coworkers on Pod People–watch!"

To most eyes, Humphrey had little reaction, but Karina noticed a slight flutter of his eyelids, an uncontrollable twitch that confirmed her suspicion.

29 House Select Committee on Intelligence and Senate Select Committee on Intelligence.

Humphrey fidgeted a bit as he unlocked his office door and led her in.

"Young lady, I have no idea why you would make such an accusation—"

As they entered the doorway, they were shocked to find a man behind Humphrey's desk, having already removed most of the drawers and turned them upside down, scattering the contents around the room. As they entered, he didn't look surprised or even embarrassed, just irritated.

"Who the devil are you and what are you doing in my office?" exclaimed Humphrey.

Karina greeted the man with an exasperated sigh. "Alec."

"You know him?"

"Partner."

"Husband," the man behind the desk corrected.

"You're going through my desk!" Humphrey realized.

"He's observant," Alec said to Karina, ignoring the fuming Humphrey. "That's probably why he's in charge. So far I haven't found anything that corroborates what he told Congress."

"That drawer was locked!" Humphrey roared indignantly.

"Yes, and badly," Alec said, folding up a switchblade. Unlike the well-put-together Karina, Alec wore a black leather jacket, black collared shirt, and blue jeans.

"Very subtle, Alec," fumed Karina. "I was just asking him—"

"You have no right to break into my—how did you even get in here, anyway?"

"I'm the CIA, Mr. Humphrey," Alec confirmed with a particularly unclassified glee, and leaped over the desk in rather overdramatic fashion. "We blow up more before 9:00 a.m. than most people do all day. I've just gotten the green light to terrorize everybody who's trying to terrorize us. I'm gonna sprinkle bacon bits on their *halal* meat, tell 'em we've got moles in their networks just to freak them out and spread paranoia, hack their Web sites, and use their kaffiyehs for tablecloths. You think Spiderman-ing my way into here and finding whatever you've got on any al-Qaeda al-Kudzu is beyond me?" He nodded his head toward Humphrey's office window, open for the first time in anyone's memory.

"How did you open that?" Wilkins exclaimed. "I've been here more than twenty years; I didn't know they could open."

Karina peered out the window. Humphrey stammered with rage.

"This is . . . this is . . ."

"This is too high," declared Karina. "He didn't climb in here. Alec, you left early this morning. You probably demonstrated your traditional respect for cover by pulling rank on the Federal Protective Service guys at the front desk, then got the maintenance staff to open the door. Judging from the marks around the paint, you cut open the paint around the windows and then opened it, just so you could make Humphrey *think* you climbed up the outside wall and broke in here so he would think you're some James Bond cat-burglar type instead of a hyperactive analyst itching to discover some yet-unnoticed threat. Besides being borderline illegal, I think this sort of intimidation is utterly unnecessary."

Alec rolled his eyes. "Do you yell out how the magic tricks work at David Copperfield shows, too?" He turned to Humphrey.

"Look, Humph, it's a whole new world and guys like me have been given free rein to go find bad people and hurt them in any way we want. All the old rules are out the window."

"Including the Fourth Amendment, it would seem," sniffed Humphrey.

"If you've got anything that points to some . . . invasive

locust attack or something, I've gotta know. And the clock is ticking, Bub. I'm a busy man, I've got places to be and important people to kill."

"I'm afraid I could never share such sensitive information without authorization through proper channels."

Alec stared at Humphrey incredulously, then looked beyond him to Karina.

"Honey, I need to smash something on his desk to make a dramatic and vaguely threatening gesture. What's important enough, but not too expensive?"

"He's already admitted as much, there's nothing to the claims," Karina sighed. "I could see it in his eyes. He doesn't want to lie to me, but he doesn't want to admit he's spreading lies to Congress, so he's stalling for time. Let's go, Alec. Real CIA officers don't spend their time berating bureaucrats. Only analysts who have been pressed into field duty because of an extraordinary national emergency do things like that," she teased.

Alec rolled his eyes and pointed a finger at Humphrey, Wilkins, and Carla.

"You will see me again," he promised.

. . .

For Ava, the job offer came through just in time.

The consulting firm, Abartmak & Associates, had been founded by a pair of immigrants and had rapidly grown in the past decade. Although still smaller than the bigger-name firms like Deloitte, Booz Allen, and KPMG, they had been starting to expand beyond their primary client base of government agencies and departments. In the past year they had picked up Oceanic Airlines and Weyland-Yutani.

"I knew I wanted to come back to D.C., and that would be

the case even if Silicon Valley didn't have about a million people just like me looking for work," she said. Ava sat in the office of an elegant Latina, Esmerelda Alves. The office's occupant was technically Ava's new boss, but Ava knew she would see her rarely.

"Our luck, then," said Alves. "When we saw your combination of government and dot-com experience, we knew we had someone who we could instantly use in our work with government database analysis, consulting, security, and upgrade planning. We've had a boom since—well, you know—and obviously we face new complications in . . . bringing in employees from overseas."

Ava nodded.

"With security on everyone's mind, every government agency is rethinking things, and besides the planters and security keycards and such, there's new focus on database security," Esmerelda said. "Right now, we want to put you on this new contract that just came in, some small agency within the Department of Agriculture that deals with weeds."

Ava let out a long, long sigh.

10

MARCH 2003
U.S. National Debt: $6.4 trillion
Budget, USDA Agency of Invasive Species: $225.4 million

Congressman Vernon Hargis of West Virginia, seventy-four and now among the highest-ranking Democrats on the House Appropriations Committee, was one of the very few individuals in Washington that had Adam Humphrey's direct line. The era of cellular phones greatly complicated Humphrey's philosophy of strategic unavailability.

But Humphrey understood that he needed a smooth relationship with Vernon Hargis more intensely than he needed some of his internal organs, and so he always answered Hargis's calls immediately, on any line. Year by year, the congressman's demands grew more insistent, and the pleasantries dwindled.

And one morning, they stopped completely. Humphrey's direct line rang as he reviewed the next fiscal year's budget request for the Domer's Gulch, Kentucky–based National Center for Crop Duster Security.

He answered his phone to hear, "You tell that son of a bitch Steiner that if he doesn't find a nice, right cushy job for my boy

Austin, that I'll squeeze his funding so hard that his ballies will pop like grapes!" the congressman barked.

Humphrey paused, contemplating his options. The congressman, increasingly erratic, was clearly enraged; "Steiner" undoubtedly referred to Conrad Steiner, the head of the most prominent pesticide producers association in the United States. Humphrey had heard rumblings of some sort of discontent over at that organization in recent months, but nothing specific.

"Just a moment, Congressman, permit me to get a pen," Humphrey said, ignoring Hargis's comfort with using him as a messaging service. "The term *ballies* has two *l*s, correct?"

"I mean it, Humphrey, that little piss-ant just turned me down like I was a no-name freshman ranked last on the District subcommittee!" the congressman continued to fume. "Nobody talks to me like that! And after all these years, to just blow me off like I'm some nobody!"

"Congressman, I'm afraid I'm not quite up to speed on this matter," Humphrey said. "What, in particular, did he turn down? And am I correct that 'Austin' is your deputy chief of staff Jacob Austin?"

After he calmed some, Hargis explained that after a decade of loyal service, his deputy chief of staff was seeking private employment with the Greater American Society of Pesticide Producers, or GASPP, an industry association and lobbying group that represented an $11 billion industry.

Hargis and GASPP had enjoyed a happy and mutually beneficial relationship for decades, but suddenly when one of Hargis's favorite employees had sought a job in "policy analysis and legislative outreach"—more commonly known to the general public as "lobbying"—he had failed to score an interview and found his phone calls unreturned.

. . .

"Wait, where are you going?" Wilkins whined in response to Humphrey's announcement of his sudden departure. "We have afternoon meetings lined up like planes landing at Dulles!"

"Cancel them!" Humphrey ordered in an uncharacteristically gruff manner. "I have to prevent a war."

"A little late, boss, unless you know some secret to motivating Saddam Hussein," Wilkins said.

"Not that war, the one between Hargis and our friends in the pesticide industry." He grabbed his raincoat and umbrella and headed toward the door. But after a few steps, he suddenly stopped, and glanced across the room at the television.

The cable news network's coverage of imminent war had briefly interrupted for an update on the day's most bizarre development: a man wearing a military helmet and displaying an upside-down American flag had driven a John Deere tractor into a shallow pond in Constitution Gardens, near the Vietnam Veterans Memorial Wall. The man had claimed to have explosives, and threatened to blow himself up if police approached him.[30]

Humphrey watched the breathless coverage of the crisis just down the street for a few moments, and then sighed.

"Wilkins, Farmer McVeigh over there, just outside our offices—is he one of ours?"

"Nope. He's protesting the end of federal tobacco subsidies."

"Ah," Humphrey exhaled relief. "Carry on, then."

30 This strange threat and standoff indeed occurred about a day before the Iraq War began. As Wikipedia summarizes, "The U.S. Park Police cordoned off a large area on the Mall extending from the Lincoln Memorial to the Washington Monument. Several nearby government offices were also evacuated and major traffic arteries in the area were closed, which caused massive jams and paralyzed traffic across the Washington metropolitan area for four consecutive rush hours." He kept the police away for forty-seven hours, then surrendered and was sentenced to sixteen months in prison.

. . .

A half hour later, Humphrey found himself in the luxurious office of Conrad Steiner, president of GASPP. At least one forest had been clear-cut to provide the wood in the ornate bookshelves lining the walls, and the desk, mostly empty, appeared to be best measured in acres. Humphrey looked around and realized his office desperately needed an upgrade in furniture.

"Conrad, I consider diplomacy to be a key facet of my role at my agency, but I'm fighting a cold, everyone's on edge about reprisal attacks for war in the Middle East, and some yokel on a tractor is threatening to blow himself up outside my office if the government stops paying him to grow a crop that kills people, so you'll find me at less than peak diplomatic sensitivity today," Humphrey began.

"Let's hear it, Humphrey," Steiner said, reclining in a chair that used more leather than the Folsom Street Fair.

"Why in the devil's name are you not hiring Jacob Austin?"

Steiner had clearly expected the question, and spoke simply, as if rehearsed.

"He's not qualified."

"That is absolute nonsense, as the only qualification any lobbyist needs is access,"[31] Humphrey scoffed. "Do you truly believe a former deputy chief of staff to a high-ranking member of the Appropriations Committee can't get his phone calls returned?"

Steiner sighed. He turned his computer monitor toward Humphrey and typed in a URL: kstreetproject.com.

A Web site popped up on the screen.

"It's a lobbying database," Steiner said. "Keeps track of

31 Continetti, *The K Street Gang,* p. 50.

lobbyists' employment histories, partisan leanings, and, of course, donations."[32]

"I'm familiar with it," Humphrey nodded. "It's run by . . . by . . ." The name escaped Humphrey's memory. "The short Viking who's always going on about taxes."

"Grover Norquist. The scorecard of who gets hired to do what has traditionally been . . . low profile," Steiner explained. "Norquist makes sure everybody knows who gets hired by whom, and DeLay and his lieutenants in the House are . . . not subtle about whether they approve. They and some of the other biggies, NFIB, U.S. Chamber of Commerce, etc., meet every Thursday. Santorum holds similar meetings on the Senate side. And every time one of our guys or I meet with them, the message is pretty clear: 'Play ball with us, don't play ball with them.'"

Humphrey shrugged. "I'll use a golf metaphor so a lobbyist like yourself can understand: Isn't that fairly par for the course?"

"Thirty-three of the top thirty-six top-level lobbying positions open in the last year have gone to Republicans."

"Good, our Republican friends are acclimating to the capital's habitat," Humphrey said. "They'll stop trying to throw sand in the gears and get with the program."

"Yeah, well, right now they're getting even better at it than the Democrats were," Steiner replied. "You ever run into that guy Gully? He's like the mob enforcer over there. I keep asking where they dug him up, because I'm pretty sure he's a ghoul or zombie or something."

"I highly doubt that," Humphrey said with a straight face. "Zombies subsist on brains, and surely on Capitol Hill the poor beast would starve."

32 Continetti, *The K Street Gang*, p. 45.

Drake Gully seemed to rotate among the staffs of the House Republican leaders from year to year, and generally projected one of the most menacing visages and demeanors on Capitol Hill, an impression only vaguely mitigated by his slight lisp.

Steiner chuckled. "If I hire Austin, I've got big problems with the majority, and hatchet men like Gully will make me pay for God knows how long. I know you're here because Hargis is irate; he called me and left fourteen voice messages. Apparently when he put his phone in his pocket, he kept accidentally hitting redial."

"You'll have to forgive the congressman, he's not used to phones."

Steiner laughed. "That's because when he was first elected, they still used the Pony Express."

. . .

Every once in a while, after a particularly difficult week, Humphrey and Wilkins would tell their wives that they would be late, and headed off to the bar at the Willard InterContinental hotel on Pennsylvania Avenue.

Wilkins had finished his first brown liquor when he exclaimed, "Adam, why does it seem like the hiring of one guy is the fate of the world for us?"

"Because it's a priority to Congressman Hargis," sighed Humphrey.

"You realize he's losing his marbles, right?" Wilkins asked. "The last time I spoke to him, he referred to Cheney as the Defense Secretary."

"We're at war with Iraq, the president is named Bush, and that burly Austrian is making another killer robot movie," Humphrey said. "I think some historical confusion is forgivable."

" 'Historical confusion'? Adam, Hargis is going senile!"

"Perhaps." Humphrey shrugged. "But thankfully as a congressman, he's in an environment where few will notice and it will have minimal impact on his work."

"We're in the very best of hands." Wilkins rolled his eyes. "You know he's hapless without his staff. At some point we should eliminate the middleman and just have the congressional chiefs of staffs cast the votes. It would be a bit fairer, since the staffers do most of the work. Let the voters know who's really calling the shots."

"Oh, life for the Hill staffers is fairer than it used to be," Humphrey said. "Sure, they're young, working exceptionally long hours, could lose their jobs at any time if their boss is defeated or keels over, but at least now they have the promise of a payoff after a distinguished period of service."

"Nobody goes to work on Capitol Hill to get rich," retorted Wilkins.

"No, but how long can you work modest five-figures and no job security, surrounded by those in the finest of suits and the Burberry scarf, the Cartier leather briefcase, the glint of light shining off their Rolex, heading off to their expense-account lunches at the Palm or the Monocle? Oh, that's right, there's a gift ban for staffers—we can't even pick up the check for lunch. The average salary for a lobbyist is three hundred thousand dollars, and lobbying the government is a two-billion-dollar-per-year industry. It's only fair that hardworking congressional staffers be given a chance to enjoy a piece of the pie."

. . .

On Capitol Hill, the increasingly haggard Congressman Nick Bader was attempting to end a meeting with some wunderkind former Health and Human Services undersecretary who was about to launch a quixotic bid to run for governor of Louisiana. The young policy wonk was undoubtedly bright and knew his policy backward and forward, but Bader could barely understand him, between his unimaginably fast speaking pace and his unexpectedly thick Louisiana drawl. He contemplated recording the aspiring governor's remarks and later playing it back at half speed, just to make sure he understood him correctly.

"Well, look, I've really got to get to this committee hearing," Bader said, picking up his pace and hoping the skinny Indian-American couldn't walk as fast as he spoke. "I think you've got some great ideas, and I'll be happy to help you out with a fundraiser or something, but I'll warn you, I've been here a long time and changing the way Washington works is a hell of a—"

"OfcourseinWashingtonhistoryalwaysrepeatsitself;that's whywehavetobepromotingreformsinthestatesandtheroleof freemarketreformmindedallieslikeyourselfistoensurethat thefederalbureaucracydoesntgetintheway;believemeIknow howhardthiscanbewhenIwasatHHSIkeptrunningintobrick wallafterbrickwallsometimesoutofstatusquosometimesout ofresistancetoconservativeeffortstobringmarketplaceforcesto healthcarearenaandIthinksomeofitwasjustasenseorperhapsa hopethatiftheyignoredmeIwouldgoaway;ImeanIwasmuch youngerthanmostundersecretariesandnobodycouldbelieveI hadalreadyruntheLouisianaDepartmentofHealthandHospitals inadditiontoabipartisancommissiononthefutureofMedicare andtheLouisianaUniversitySystem," the aspiring governor began.

The meeting would have gone on forever if the pair hadn't nearly walked into a tall, pale, menacing figure in a black suit, Drake Gully. The gaunt staffer for the House Republican leadership glared briefly at the man occupying Bader's attention.

"Catch ya later," Bobby Jindal said, and he disappeared down the hall.

Bader, however, had seen Gully's conversational intimidation techniques before and was unimpressed. "My day just gets better and better," he said with a roll of the eyes. "So what do *you* want?"

A lesser man might be ashamed of his lisp, but Drake Gully made it work for him.

"We could ussse your asssistansss . . ." Gully began. "Our friendsss are hearing that Hargisss is attempting to get one of hisss former ssstaffers into the lobbying ssshop of the pesssticide producersss . . ." He put a long, skinny arm around Bader's back. "We need to reinforss the message to industriesss like thisss one that they should be always thinking of our . . . Republican friendsss and their ssstaffersss firssst."

"Oh, you mean your noble crusade to end the unbearable injustice that not enough of the good lobbying jobs are going to Republican staffers, huh?"

"Pre-sssisssely."

Bader wriggled out from Gully's attempted reacharound. He was tempted to imitate Gully's *s* hisses, but thought better of it. "I'm going to say this slowly, so that even you can understand," Bader jeered. "When I look at the gargantuan monstrosity that is our federal government, and the disaster that is Washington, the absolute last problem on my mind is that not enough of our staffers are getting cushy perches in Gucci Gulch!"

"Thisss iss a priority for *Majority Leader* DeLay," Gully said emphatically.

"I can't believe any majority leader worth the title would spend one frickin' minute worrying about penny ante crap like this!" Bader exclaimed, eyes bulging. "What the hell do I care about who hires who? I thought the whole point of our side was that we didn't want the government meddling in that stuff! Jesus Christ, we're going to war, we're on alert for al-Qaeda, the debt's over six trillion dollars, and you're worried about who gets to sit in the nicest booth at the Palm?"

"Your lack of cooperation with our requessst will be . . . noted," Gully said threateningly.

"You note that, and then you take that note, and stick it up your—"

Gully, offended, turned away.

But Bader remained indignant. "You tell him if he keeps focusing on crap like this, there won't be a majority to lead!"

• • •

Humphrey was beaming the next time he appeared in Steiner's K Street office, a few weeks later.

"I have a solution," Humphrey said.

"I thought you might," Steiner said warily. "Let's hear it."

Humphrey leaned forward and gave a confident smile. "Pay him."

Steiner threw up his hands. "Then I incur the wrath of DeLay, Norquist, and the rest. Can't do it."

"I didn't say *hire* him, I said *pay* him." Humphrey raised an eyebrow, pleased with his own cleverness, but Steiner just looked at Humphrey in absolute incomprehension.

"You mean hire him to do some other non-lobbying job?" Steiner asked.

"Oh!" Humphrey brought a fist to his mouth. "That could work, too! But considering the risk that DeLay and his K Street Goon Squad might object to him having any *actual* duties, I think the best option is to simply pay him and not have him do any actual . . . work."

"Why would I pay somebody to not work? That's insane."

"Do you know how many farmers are paid by the government not to farm in order to ensure price stability?"

Steiner's balding mug contorted from incredulity to a stifled outrage. "I am not going to pay a six-figure salary to somebody to just stay away from the office! Even I have to justify my expenses!" He pounded a fist on the desk, but Humphrey just gave him an oh-come-now look.

"I mean, periodically!"

Humphrey wouldn't give up the sales pitch. "Conrad, how many parties are represented on Capitol Hill?"

"Are you going to give me the Bernie-Sanders-is-technically-a-Socialist speech again?"

"There are three parties—the Democrats, the Republicans, and the Appropriators, and that last one is, far and away, more powerful than the others. Surely, the happiness and continued cooperation of Congressman Hargis—a man capable of steering *billions* in government spending!—is worth a modest six-figure sum. Think of the return on investment! Hiring Austin for a modest $110,000 per year or so simply makes good business sense!"

Steiner sat back in his chair. "This is stupid."

"This is the price of doing business."

Humphrey smiled as Conrad Steiner let out a long, resigned sigh, a signal his opposition was rapidly evaporating.

11

AUGUST 2006

U.S. National Debt: $8.5 trillion

Budget, USDA Agency of Invasive Species: $257.8 million

N o one knows precisely why terrible things happen, or why so many warning signs get ignored.

Many of the 9/11 hijackers ran into U.S. law enforcement multiple times before the attacks—mostly getting speeding tickets and citations for failure to produce a driver's license— but only Zacarias Moussaoui was locked within a prison cell on that awful September day.

Germany's intelligence service claims that it warned the U.S. government that they doubted the credibility of one of their key sources on the Iraqi programs for weapons of mass destruction, an Iraqi defector code-named "Curveball."

New Orleans had an evacuation plan, but city officials scrapped it as Hurricane Katrina bore down upon the city in 2005.

And in 2006, a wind blew north from Mexico. A rare and unexpected variation of the periodic weather pattern El Niño, known as La Suegra, sent winds up from the Baja Peninsula across the southern border into California.

That spring, Mexico's northern territories had a particularly virulent strain of a weed called "cheatgrass" blooming. The common name cheatgrass comes from western farmers who thought they had been given impure seed when the weed appeared in fields. The weed, also known as drooping brome, had been present in nearly every state for years, but was largely manageable; cheatgrass is an annual—it lives for only one year/ growing season and then dies.

However, as weeds go, cheatgrass is a pain in the *tuchus*. It has no natural biological predators. It sucks away water and moisture with a ruthless efficiency, squeezing out the roots of other plants. The weed is highly flammable and exacerbates the risk of wildfires.

And in the summer of 2006, it cropped up all over the farms of California. Ordinarily, this would be a high-priority matter for both the U.S. Department of Agriculture's Agency of Invasive Species and its state-level equivalent.

But part of the problem came from the name of the Golden State's band of weed watchmen, the California Regional Invasive Species Information System, known as CRISIS.[33]

Many of the memos sent from the U.S. Department of Agriculture's field offices in California referred to the reports as a "crisis," and when the initial memos generated little response in Washington, concerned USDA employees e-mailed that it was a "CRISIS!" Of course, the Agency of Invasive Species employees in Washington scanning the e-mail headers thought it was simply referring to the acronym.

Memos were ignored. Meetings proceeded at the regular pace.

Meanwhile, the spores continued to be carried by the wind, settling on the farms and fields of the Golden State, and letting

33 No, I'm not making this up. The state agency's acronym really is CRISIS.

their little roots settle into the soil. In time, those roots started digging down and grabbing every bit of water they could.

Within weeks, it was clear that the cheatgrass epidemic was going to have a particularly deleterious effect on two of California's most important, indeed iconic, crops: the grapes of wine country and marijuana. Entrepreneurial-minded craftsmen of the other "weed" had taken to growing large fields of marijuana in the least-traveled corners of state, national, and public parklands, lands that state and federal lawmakers had loudly insisted must be kept off-limits to drilling or other forms of economic exploitation. While the oil and natural gas companies honored the regulations they deemed so wrongheaded, a small army of marijuana growers used the lands to generate millions in profitable crops, entirely tax-free.

Outside California, the cheatgrass crisis was mostly lost in the shuffle of screaming headlines about a series of natural and manmade disasters: Hurricane Katrina's devastation on the Gulf Coast, increasing casualties in Iraq, the collapse of a mine in West Virginia, the demotion of Pluto from the ranks of the planets, and the nomination of Harriet Miers to the Supreme Court.

For the wine crop, consumers noticed a couple dollars' increase in bottles; for a while Trader Joe's customers griped about the sudden appearance of "Four Buck Chuck."

The sudden spike in marijuana prices also spurred a little-remembered Snoop Dogg lyric:

> *Don't know who's behind this dirty deed*
> *Somebody's jackin' up the price of my weed*

While the story was largely ignored outside California, across the country, late-night copy editors rejoiced at the opportunity to use "weed" puns in headlines.

SEPTEMBER 2006

House Minority Leader Nancy Pelosi was asked by a California reporter whether she felt the federal government was responding sufficiently to the cheatgrass woes of farmers in her home state.

"No, no, not at all, and it's another failure of this administration," Pelosi said, her face frozen in an expression of wide-eyed shock and horror. "This just shows that we need to create a federal agency to be on alert for the threat of invasive species."

At that precise moment, separately, on opposite sides of Independence Avenue, Agency of Invasive Species Administrative Director Adam Humphrey and Congressman Nicholas Bader choked on their lunches.

· · ·

"Are you kidding me?" Bader exclaimed to a Republican colleague whom he deemed insufficiently enraged about Pelosi's comment. "They've been around since the Carter years, and Pelosi didn't even know they existed!"

His colleague shrugged. "There are a lot of things Nancy Pelosi doesn't know."

Bader shook his head. "No, what I mean is, here's a government agency with one friggin' stupid little mission, and they completely dropped the ball on it. Actually, they didn't just drop the ball, they Bucknered it!"

"So you want to grill the agency's managers?"

"I want to throw their shiftless, unaccountable bodies on a Foreman Grill, yes," Bader said. "Watch them sizzle and pop."

"Talk to Carrington. He's on the Oversight committee, and he's the member whose district would probably be most affected by all this."

Bader groaned at the thought.

Congressman Theodore Roosevelt Carrington and Bader had served in Congress together for twelve years, but had barely spoken. Bader was a suburban budget hawk, always banging on about pork and earning accolades from the Cato Institute and other small-government groups, hanging with folks like Ron Paul of Texas, Floyd Flake of New York, Bobby Jindal of Louisiana, and in earlier Congresses, Pat Toomey of Pennsylvania, Tom Coburn of Oklahoma, and Mark Sanford of South Carolina.

Carrington ranked among the chamber's least conservative Republicans, with a lifetime American Conservative Union rating of 51.102 out of a possible 100. To the extent he associated with any of his Republican colleagues, he hung around with Mike Castle of Delaware, Tom Davis of Virginia, and Teddy Van Voorhees VII of New York.

Carrington came from the oldest of old money and had more or less inherited his seat on the reputation of his family's good name and philanthropic work in Northern California. Nicknamed "the congressman from Merlot," Carrington was the last person in the world Bader wanted as an ally on a crusade like this.

. . . .

After Pelosi's comments, the cheatgrass crisis finally got a bit more national coverage; the bottom of the front page of the *Wall Street Journal* featured one of those pointillism portraits of the weed.

"This is brutal," groaned Lisa Bloom, recently promoted to the agency's communications director.

Lisa had finally achieved that long-sought career step, and Jamie Caro-Marcus was now director of event planning, a title she enjoyed. Ava, however, told her friends she was on the verge of leaving government work for good. She had been writing freelance pieces on government policy and technology—careful to avoid reporting about anything she did at the Agency of Invasive Species, but her knowledge and outlook were clearly shaped by her day job. Payment by payment, pleased editor by pleased editor, Ava felt confident she was close to finding a full-time writing gig.

Within the sanctum of Humphey's office, Lisa and her bosses just began to grasp the public relations disaster that had suddenly befallen the agency. She read aloud the first sentence from the jump page: "State agriculture officials say that the slow-moving federal response to the cheatgrass crisis is only the latest and most dramatic example of a pattern of failures from the USDA's Agency of Invasive Species."

"Mrs. Bloom, since the day you walked through our door, you wanted to be fully engaged in the battle of public communication. Now, you have your wish," Humphrey said, almost teasing. "Drop everything else you're doing and begin coming up with an action plan to . . . mitigate all this."

There was a knock at the office and Wilkins popped his head in with a distinctly uneasy look.

"I see our fact-finding mission has garnered our traditionally disastrous results," sighed Humphrey.

. . .

Wilkins closed the door behind him and spoke in a hushed, terrified tone.

"Humphrey . . . we screwed up."

"How bad?"

"Think of the *Hindenburg* . . . crashing into the *Titanic* . . . as it sails to Pompeii . . . with Ford Pintos sent to rescue the wounded."

"Calm down and tell me everything you've learned."

"I didn't write anything down, as you instructed—okay, I wrote it on my hands."

"Good. The last thing we need are any ... unflattering memos or other paperwork to be requested by Congress or FOIAed."

"Everything that has ever bothered me about this place joined forces just as this cheatgrass wave was coming up from Mexico. The complacency, the miscommunication or lack of communication, the lack of urgency, the pervasive belief that somebody else out there was taking care of the problem, the human cholesterol of incompetent staff that were too much trouble to fire, everyone waiting for approval from everyone else before taking actions, the endless meetings, the postponed meetings, the rescheduled meetings, the missed meetings, the memos that went unread, the e-mails that were 'skimmed'—I swear to God, the next time I need to tell people something, I'm posting it above the urinals and on the bathroom stall doors."

"So you're saying our staff missed red flags," Humphrey said uneasily.

"It was a friggin' Turkish army parade, Adam!" Wilkins was furious. "Every farmer in California was finding these things and reporting them! They didn't get noticed because there was a backlog of old reports piling up! When people did start passing the reports up the chain, everybody acted like it was just another day at the office, instead of the ... the ... the Pearl Harbor of weeds!"

Humphrey stood for a moment, trying to grasp the enormity of the foul-up now detailed in marker ink up and down his assistant's forearms.

"Wash your hands," Humphrey said.

. . .

The following week meant a lot of trips up to Capitol Hill for Humphrey, attempting to placate the increasingly upset voices in Congress. Quite a few members of California's delegation from agricultural districts, usually warm and friendly and eager to vote for more spending, were suddenly nasty and harsh and full of criticism.

The only bright part of the week for Humphrey was running into Congressman Nick Bader again, and another opportunity to antagonize his Reagan-era foe. But even this regularly recurring confrontation proceeded a bit differently than usual.

Humphrey spotted Bader emerging from a fundraiser at the Capitol Hill Club.

"Congressman!" Humphrey greeted him with transparently fake enthusiasm. "I suppose I should call you by that title every chance I get, since I hear the polls in Pennsylvania indicate you're hanging by a thread. You must feel so reassured with that Santorum figure, trailing by double digits and leading the charge for you atop your party's ticket!"

"Shows what an inside-the-Beltway type like you knows," Bader growled. "We've got a legendary NFL Hall of Fame Pittsburgh Steeler on the top of the ticket."[34]

"I'm sure that means so much to your district full of Philadelphia fans."

"I'll take my problems over yours, Humphrey," Bader sparred. "If I lose my seat, I know why: a war that's going on too long, exhaustion with the president, a bunch of numbskulls in my party playing footsie with Abramoff and strangling their mistresses."

"As a member of the party of family values, it offends you to see a colleague strangling a woman that isn't his wife, doesn't it?"

---

34 Former Steelers wide receiver Lynn Swann was the Republican nominee for governor in 2006.

"Laugh all ya want, Humphrey, just remember you and your whole agency have no friends in either party anymore," Bader warned. "You guys are the latest poster boys for incompetent government. The CIA, FEMA, every doofus in the Departments of Commerce and Labor, the sneaker-sniffers at TSA—they're all sighing relief right now, knowing that the walking definition of wasteful government is the Agency of Invasive Species that ignored the weed that ate California wine country."

For once, Adam Humphrey found himself groping for a snappy comeback.

NOVEMBER 2006
U.S. National Debt: $8.63 trillion

Congressman Nicholas Bader, Republican of Philadelphia's outer suburbs, shouldn't have survived the Democratic Tsunami of 2006, but somehow he hung on by about one percentage point.

Bader called in to a well-connected political junkie/talking head, a guy who always went into every election night with a thick binder of data that dissected that year's electorate in extravagant detail. Two years earlier, he had confidently projected an Ohio win for Bush well before the polls had closed, citing a personally executed exit poll by phone of the key swing streets within the key swing communities of the key swing counties in that most important of swing states. When Ned Simmons of James Street in the Eastmoor neighborhood of Columbus, a former voter for Perot, Clinton, and Gore, said that he was voting for Bush because of the way the president handled the issue of terrorism, this junkie felt confident calling Ohio for Bush, even though the polls were open for another three hours. (He predicted all states correctly except one, Wisconsin, a miss he attributed to the strange fact that seven thousand more ballots were cast in Milwaukee than the number of people recorded as voting.)

"Congratulations, Congressman."

"Thanks. Now I get to see if I'm the last of the Mohicans. How bad is it?"

"Well, they just called another race in the Midwest," the bespectacled guru answered. "By my rankings, the Democrats just knocked off the . . . the fifty-fourth most vulnerable House Republican."

Bader swore, and swore, and swore. And then he swore some more.

. . .

Morale in the office of the Agency of Invasive Species was mixed the morning after Election Day 2006. The vast majority of the staff was only too happy to kiss Republican congressional majorities good-bye, although they had encountered less and less trouble with the appropriations process each year. And while the Democrats were undoubtedly open to spending more on the Department of Agriculture as a whole (and in most departments), the cheatgrass crisis—"Weedgate," as it was called in some corners of the Internet—hadn't really gone away, and California Democrats seemed particularly irate in their criticism of the agency. The news cycle of the election season had provided plenty of distractions away from Humphrey and the AIS—*macaca!*—but there was a pervasive gloom that worse days were ahead.

Bader's unexpected skin-of-his-teeth victory was just one more disappointment to stick in the agency's collective craw.

"We almost got rid of him!" cried Wilkins. "So close! If we had just flipped about a thousand votes!"

"I'm afraid we will have Nicholas Bader to kick around for another two years," sighed Humphrey.

One of the day's key moments came in the afternoon, when a cheerful group of House Democrats held a press conference to lay out their agenda in the year to come.

Speaker-elect Nancy Pelosi and a succession of Democrats announced their intentions to investigate the Bush administration on the handling of the Iraq War, the FEMA response to Katrina, the firing of U.S. Attorneys, the ties to Jack Abramoff, and a "callous and tight-fisted" approach to Fannie Mae and Freddie Mac, making it far too difficult for ordinary Americans to get home loans.

"Finally, we believe that this administration has ill-served the American people by allowing a crisis in our agricultural community to spread unabated," Pelosi said, her eyes wide and her cheekbones taut with concern and outrage. "Tens of millions of farmers—I'm sorry, tens of thousands of farmers, and millions of American consumers, are still asking how it could happen. How could something as small and simple as a weed cause such economic and social distress? And where was the federal agency assigned with tracking this threat? How could the Department of Agriculture's Agency of Invasive Species fail in its mission so thoroughly?"

"I have spoken to Senate Majority Leader–elect Reid, and in January, Democrats in both chambers will vote to establish a bipartisan National Cheatgrass Disaster Commission, to investigate how this crisis occurred and who should be held accountable."

. . .

Within the offices of the Agency of Invasive Species, everything just stopped for a moment.

Everyone looked at each other, trying to process that their failure to respond to the cheatgrass crisis would now be the subject of a special bipartisan commission, with all that process had come to include: televised hearings, showboating commissioners, competitive leaking, and the intense, unrelenting hunt for scapegoats. Resignations demanded. Instant celebrity status.

"We're screwed," Wilkins whispered.

12

JANUARY 2007

U.S. National Debt: $8.7 trillion

Budget, USDA Agency of Invasive Species: $263.5 million

Agency of Invasive Species Administrative Director Adam Humphrey deployed the time-honored "It will distract us from our duties!" excuse to every Democrat on Capitol Hill, to no avail. With surprising speed, the House and Senate passed legislation establishing the National Cheatgrass Disaster Commission, and awaited the leaders of each party and the White House to nominate members.

After watching the final vote on C-SPAN in Humphrey's office—Lisa was starting to refer to it as "The Bunker"—Wilkins plopped down in his seat and rubbed his temples.

"They are going to crucify us," Wilkins whimpered.

"They will do no such thing," Humphrey insisted.

"Do you read the news, Adam? We waterboard people now! Crucifixion is, like, a half step away!"

. . .

The first four appointees to the commission surprised most of Washington, as the political world thought all of them had passed away ages earlier. The quartet, all long retired, had been selected for their stature, respect on both sides of the aisle, long-standing ties to the agricultural community, and everyone's well-placed faith that there was absolutely no way any of them would make waves. They made David Gergen look edgy.

Senate Republicans had appointed former Kansas senator Dorothy Abernathy and former Alabama lieutenant governor Roy Beane. Senate Democrats had appointed former California agriculture commissioner Calvin Robinson and retired Oklahoma State professor Dee Dixon. The youngest among them was Dixon at seventy-one; Beane clocked in at a spry eighty-four years of age; Abernathy and Robinson were currently residing in assisted-living communities.

"Lieutenant Governor and retired general Beane," Wilkins read off the wire service story just posted online. "Was he in the army?" he asked.

"Yes, the Confederate one," replied Humphrey.

The editorial page of the *Washington Post* delicately praised the quartet as "relics of a bygone era of bipartisan cooperation"; *The Economist* indelicately used the term "unearthed mummies" in their summary. With four of the seven slots taken up by near-late figures in the agricultural policy community, the commission's tone and direction would rest heavily on the names of the three remaining commissioners. One commissioner had yet to be selected by House Republican leadership, one by House Democrats, and the commission's chairman was to be appointed by the president, with Reid and Pelosi required to sign off.

. . .

Since his defeat in the midterms, Ted Carrington had been a changed man. He was shocked that his constituents had tossed him out in the 2006 landslide, insisting on election night that there had to be some sort of mistake. He was nothing like the Republican colleagues he had often publicly dismissed as Neanderthals, the George Allens, the Rick Santorums, the Lincoln Chafees.

His postelection interviews revealed a long-repressed rage and bitterness; one was headlined THE CONGRESSMAN FROM MERLOT TURNS VINEGARY.

Carrington once tolerated Nick Bader's strange obsession with a little-known federal agency fighting weed infestations. Now, with the passion of the converted, he began to preach the gospel of the incompetent, arrogant, out-of-touch bureaucrats of Washington, none worse than the shiftless layabouts at the Agency of Invasive Species. He greeted the formation of the National Cheatgrass Disaster Commission as near-miraculous; he proclaimed it would finally correct the record. The ruined crops, the lost wages, the economic aftershocks, the Four Buck Chuck—none of it was his fault. He had been nobly performing his public service, all along, when the useless idiots at AIS messed it all up.

Of course, Carrington had the slight fear that allies of the agency might try to pin the blame elsewhere. And so he suddenly campaigned for the job of commission member with far greater urgency, diligence, and determination than he ever put into any of his congressional races.

Bader found himself on the phone with John Boehner, the new House minority leader, desperately trying to put the most furious, newly minted critic of the Agency of Invasive Species on the special panel that would give it the public policy equivalent of a colonoscopy.

Carrington began hanging around Bader's congressional office for no particular reason, and Bader was wondering if there was a delicate way to get the U.S. Capitol Police to remove a former member. Carrington kept trying to peek in Bader's office door every time someone entered or departed.

"Boehner, you gotta put Carrington on the cheatgrass commission. He knows the stuff, he's connected with all the communities impacted by it, he's looking for a way to contribute, and by the time he's done, nobody will be blaming the president for this."

Boehner's response was not audible to those not on the line, but the tone sounded hesitant.

"John . . . I mean it, if you don't give him something to do and get him out of my hair, I may just have to shoot him. You know I'm rated an A+ by the NRA."

. . .

Wilkins did not knock before entering Humphrey's office.

"Boehner's putting Ted Carrington on the commission!" He was interrupting Humphrey and Lisa, who had been spending inordinate amounts of time together lately, desperately trying to construct a communications strategy to weather the category five media storm headed their way.

The pair's conversation instantly stopped. They had heard Carrington's name mentioned, but dismissed it as a long shot. From all appearances, John Boehner had a lot more problems to deal with than the cheatgrass commission. Wilkins tossed his BlackBerry to Humphrey.

Lisa looked pale. "Have you seen the way he's been tearing into us since he lost his seat? He'll turn that commission into the Spanish Inquisition."

"Carrington . . . I didn't expect that," mumbled Humphrey, reading the BlackBerry.

Wilkins couldn't help himself. "No one expects the Spanish Inquisition."

"I thought Carrington had campaigned for the job too transparently to ever be picked," Lisa said. "Bader must have gotten to Boehner."

Humphrey waived his hand. "How it happened is moot. Right now, we need to reach Hargis and any of our remaining friends in the House. We need to get a message to Pelosi. She needs to appoint a . . . *balancing* voice on the committee.

"Who did you have in mind?" Wilkins asked.

. . .

"Ha!"

Javier Puga had been waiting for a call like this for more than two years.

Puga had been a successful trial lawyer in Orlando, Florida, and was elected to Congress in 1998 on a platform of staunch opposition to congressional investigation of presidential sex acts. The Florida Democratic Party and DCCC were unnerved when he unexpectedly won the district's primary; as a candidate, he had only one tone, self-righteous indignation, and tended to blurt out anything that came into his mind. But he had money, was reasonably smart, and had a greasy charisma that worked on television. He easily won the swing district, carried along by the Democratic wave that year.

Puga approached Congress the way he had pursued his work in his personal injury practice, putting in the bare minimum of effort on the necessary paperwork and throwing himself into performing to any audience that would listen. Before long, he was spending more time on cable news networks than some actual show hosts, once getting into a loud argument with Sen. Chuck Schumer while the two were both trying to do live remote interviews in close proximity outside the Capitol Building.

Congressman Puga was among those most furious over the disputed 2000 election and recount, and he spent much of 2002 insisting Governor Jeb Bush would be defeated. Despite that erroneous prediction, he spent much of the next cycle assuring the Kerry campaign that Florida was in the bag. Meanwhile, his advisers were warning him that his district was growing tired of his relentless partisan fury. Shortly before a contentious resignation, one bald, glowering strategist bellowed, "Your mouth is writing checks that your district's Cook Partisan Voting Index Score can't cash!"

Bush won the state by five percentage points. Additionally, Puga's outer suburban district decided it had tired of his politics of perpetual rage, as well as stunts like calling for a congressional investigation of allegations that the president had served a plastic turkey during a visit with the troops in Iraq. ("I think this is potential grounds for impeachment, Keith," he had told the camera with a straight face.)

Puga returned to Florida, reopened his law practice, and waited for the local Democratic Party to beg him to run to win his old seat back. The state party officials seemed strangely unenthusiastic when he called, and those lunch meetings with the county party chairs kept getting postponed. He passed the time by blogging for *The Huffington Post*, doing the occasional television interview, and writing an angry polemic that didn't sell.

He was an unexpected choice for Pelosi to nominate to the National Cheatgrass Disaster Commission; the closest Puga ever came to agricultural work was a lawsuit contending a local restaurant chain's salad bars were insufficiently accessible to the handicapped. (They settled out of court.) But he instantly recognized that the commission was going to be looking at the disastrous performance of a federal agency on

Bush's watch, and Javier Puga knew exactly where the buck should stop.

. . .

When Bader heard Puga had been selected to the commission, he kicked a wastepaper basket across his office.

He had already talked with the White House staff about their search for a chair; they had worried that the Cheatgrass Commission (CheatComm in White House memos) would turn into a witch hunt, and one more source of headlines designed to embarrass the administration. With Carrington on board, they felt they had at least one voice that would be focusing attention on the career employees of the agency itself, and not any of Bush's appointees at the Department of Agriculture.

For a few weeks, Bader contemplated resigning his seat and leading the commission, leading his crusade right to Humphrey's doorstep. But he knew that Reid and Pelosi would probably object, even if his resignation would open up a very competitive special election in a swing district.

The addition of Puga altered the equation and made Bader's chairmanship an impossibility. Now the commission was indisputably politicized, and even floating Bader's name would inevitably bring charges that the administration was appointing its allies to ensure a cover-up.

The administration needed someone who would ensure Puga's runaway personality and showboating didn't dominate the proceedings. They needed someone respected, someone who could command a room, someone who had the authority to shut up Puga with a glare but who wasn't seen as a Bush administration ally.

Bader had just the person.

. . .

Bader found his man reading on his front porch.

Caleb Gunning Lyon was not a friend of Bader's, but a constituent. Bader had known him for years, and been starry-eyed through their first meetings, but over time found Lyon's personality inexplicably cold and prickly.

Despite his occasionally standoffish personality, Lyon remained one of Pennsylvania's most popular residents.

As a young man, Lyon had served in the Marines, was deployed to Lebanon, and helped assist the victims of the barracks bombing. His picture appeared on the cover of *Time* magazine, helping carry a wounded man. After serving, he earned his PhD in American history with extensive background in classical history, after which he became a high school teacher. His memoir/history book, *Hard Times, Hard Decisions,* became a surprise bestseller, and he bought a small orchard in Washington Crossing. He had no interest in politics, but accepted an appointment to a gubernatorial commission reviewing the state's education system. He was supposed to be a token teacher/celebrity, but wrote a scathing dissent to the main report, which he dismissed as "complacent bromides." Lyon called for rigorous standards and an emphasis on values of the Founding Fathers, which proved wildly popular and had him on *Nightline* for several nights. The governor who appointed him was facing a tough reelection fight, and he begged Lyon to accept the nomination for lieutenant governor. (The previous lieutenant governor had announced a surprise resignation to deal with "personal matters." Despite salacious rumors, the personal matter was that he had concluded he wasn't making enough money.)

Lyon was credited with being a key factor in a narrow win, even if his speeches were derided as hokey and corny, punctuating his remarks with the recurring question, "What would the Founding Fathers do?" He quietly served as lieutenant governor for two and a half years until the governor suddenly was invited by the president to Washington to accept a nomination to one of the nicer cabinet posts. Lyon became the state's most unlikely chief executive, and was the subject of some jokes as "the accidental governor." But after two months on the job, a Pittsburgh steel mill's ceiling collapsed, trapping a dozen workers. Lyon raced to the scene and actually helped direct the rescue efforts—"this is how we did it in Beirut, boys"—and when all of the workers were rescued, Lyon's approval rating hit 90 percent and stayed there for weeks.

Jay Leno called. The president called. *60 Minutes* called. Everyone adored him . . . and then Lyon announced he had no plans to run for reelection. Declaring that he believed in the American tradition of citizen-statesmen, he said his modest future plan was to return to his orchard in Washington Crossing and teach in the local high school again.

Cynics mocked the decision as a pose. The national party chairman had visited him and begged him to consider running for president.

But it wasn't a pose; Lyon shared the public's innate suspicion and distrust of the political process.

Time went by. Caleb Gunning Lyon became just a fond memory for most. President Bush called regularly, and Lyon turned down just about every invitation to every cabinet post, ambassadorship, or other bauble offered by ambitious politicians hoping some of Lyon's popularity would rub off on them.

Bader's Lincoln Town Car drove up the driveway of Lyon Orchard. He emerged, but Lyon remained sitting on the porch, barely glancing at his visitor.

"Do you prefer to be addressed as Governor Lyon or Captain Lyon?" Bader asked, smiling.

"Depends upon the culture," Lyon said, not looking up from

his book. "Colin Powell preferred to be introduced as 'Retired General Powell' on diplomatic missions to the Middle East, because that title carried more weight in Arab cultures. Secretaries of state, like governors, know how to talk. Retired generals, like captains, know how to fight." He finally looked his visitor in the eyes. "What do you want, Nick?"

Bader stepped up onto the porch.

"I hear Karl Rove asked you to chair this new Cheatgrass Disaster Commission," Bader said.

"Yup." Bader waited for more, but Lyon just continued reading and ignoring him.

After an awkward silence, Bader cleared his throat. "You probably feel like you don't need that kind of grief and aggravation. And you don't. But I'd like you to think about something before you decide."

Lyon finally looked up with something resembling actual attention.

"You sense that cynicism out there. Everybody's wailing about Iraq and Abramoff and Katrina, but it's been out there for a long while—the Chinese money in Clinton's coffers, Sandy Berger stuffing classified documents in his socks, Enron, Torricelli, the pardon sales. Iran-Contra. The Keating Five. Abscam. The bounced checks. Everybody thinks the federal government is packed to the gills with crooks and morons."

"Everybody might be correct, Congressman," Lyon said tersely.

"Well, I know it'll never get any better if we never demand any better," Bader shot back. "You know, everybody thinks you're so frigging terrific, sitting here on your porch and quoting George Washington. I think you love this precious little reputation, a hero beloved by all during a divided time, and you're scared to get your hands dirty."

Lyon reacted like he had been slapped. He slammed down

his book and his eyes glared with indignation. "Are you questioning my courage, son?"

"Yes, *Governor*, I am," Bader said. "Last year we watched a federal agency completely fail in its core mission. There's an opportunity, right here and now, to get answers, to hold people accountable, to make sure it doesn't happen again, to fix something so that government works the way it's supposed to!" He pounded a porch strut. "Everybody thinks I'm some sort of antigovernment ideological nut-job. I just want government to do its job! Sometimes I'm not even sure if I count as right-wing anymore; I still have this naïve idea that the federal government ought to do what it's supposed to do, considering what we pay for it."

Bader looked away, unsure if his brief flaring of temper was persuading Lyon or just alienating him.

"I hear from so many constituents how they wish you would run for something—governor again, or senator, or president," Bader continued. "I tell them I agree. But if you won't do this— one chairmanship, of one commission, to conduct one investigation, to try to solve one problem . . . well, I'll start telling people what I really think. That you can't be bothered with this country anymore."

That was enough to get Lyon out of his chair.

"Hold it right there, you son of a bitch!" he growled, jabbing a finger right at Bader's face in a dramatic manner that would impress veteran emphatic pointers like Harrison Ford. For a moment, Bader wondered if he was about to be decked by a retired Marine captain. Lyon stepped uncomfortably close, glared, and looked up and down at Bader.

"You have a hell of a lot of nerve coming here and talking to me like that," Lyon fumed.

"It is . . . probably not one of my better days for constituent outreach," Bader quipped.

Lyon's stern face cracked, and he unleashed a roaring laugh so deep it made James Earl Jones sound like Woody Woodpecker.

"Bader, I pretty much want to deal with politicians and Washington like I want a case of the crabs," he hoisted up his belt. "But I'll do this. One year. I'm not relocating to Washington; I'll commute on the train. And then I'm done with you people for good."

Bader smiled and extended his hand. "Let me be the first to thank you for this service, *Captain*."

. . .

Wilkins stared at the computer screen headline on *The Drudge Report*, and physically backed away. He zombie-walked over to Humphrey's office, knocked, and opened to see Lisa and the administrative director attempting to organize a small mountain of paperwork they would soon be releasing, 8½-by-11 photocopied chaff to distract and disorient the heat-seeking missiles of the press and commission investigators.

"Caleb Lyon's chairing the commission," he said, half dazed, half disbelieving.

This time it was Humphrey who stopped, put down the piece of paper, looked at Wilkins, inhaled to say something, and then didn't.

"Who's he?" Lisa asked. "I figured Bush would try to sneak Henry Kissinger or . . . who are the guys he appoints to everything? Um . . . oh, you know, Chertoff or Khalilzad."

"Caleb Lyon," sighed Wilkins, "is like Colin Powell, Norman Schwarzkopf, David McCullough, and Jaime Escalante rolled into one. The investigation of the biggest screw-up of our lives is going to be conducted by Captain America. We might as well type up our resignation letters now."

Humphrey let out a long, long sigh, and his head drooped.

Wilkins had never seen his friend and mentor this close to emotional and physical capitulation.

"Lisa," Humphrey said quietly. "We're going to have to organize a very effective, very fast-moving, and very relentless campaign of strategic leaks."

. . .

The commission held its first meeting in office space on K Street rented by the General Services Administration.

Lyon had insisted that the main conference room be cleared of staff; he wanted the commissioners to meet without entourages or an audience. Two commissioners arrived early, and Lyon was not surprised which ones. They stared at each other with no feigned collegiality or warmth; they sized each other up like street fighters.

"Congressman Puga."

"Congressman Carrington."

Lyon awaited further conversation, but none came. He was comfortable with silence, and so the three sat for five minutes without saying anything.

Finally, the other appointees to the Cheatgrass Disaster Commission—nicknamed the Four Fogeys by the disreputable whippersnappers of the blogosphere—arrived via wheelchair and walker and cane and settled into the large conference table.

Lyon had gone through some cursory introductions when the youngest member offered the first bone of contention.

"I presume the commission will be providing each of us with an office, secretary, and driver," Puga interrupted.

"No."

"What do you mean, 'no'?"

"I didn't think two little letters could be so confusing," Lyon responded with a raised eyebrow. "We have this rented office space and a small group of nonpartisan staffers. We have communal office workspace and equipment available. You'll be in charge of getting yourself here."

Puga's face was a fireworks display of disbelief, indignation, disappointment, anger, and pouting.

"I want to be clear from the beginning," Lyon began the only part of the meeting he had really looked forward to, discussing and/or lecturing the commission members about duty and patriotism. "We are charged with the responsibility of investigating a tragic and all-too-easily overlooked disaster for this country's farmers and consumers. There are two things that could ruin our efforts instantly. First, any leaks of information before we have completed our investigation. If we're seen as leaking, that will give everyone an excuse to not cooperate. Second, while partisanship in this town is off the charts, and I have no doubt we will have disagreements among us, we need to work as a unified force, a small strike team for truth, getting to the bottom of why that agency failed to—"

"Objection, Mr. Chairman!" Puga blurted out.

"This is not a court of law, Javier," Lyon growled. "What is it?

"You described our mission as getting to the bottom of why the *agency* failed, and it is a prejudicial definition, because it presumes that fault properly lies at the feet of that entity."

"Alright, Javier, how would you prefer we described our mission?"

"Well, I would begin by saying simply we must get to the bottom of *who* failed, not merely why, since my initial examination suggests the preponderance of the evidence indicates that the fault lies not with the agency, but with Bush and Rove and the other nutzos in the White House—."[35]

35 "Bush and Rove and the nutzos at the White House" was how 9/11 Commission member Max Cleland, a Democratic senator from Georgia who lost his reelection bid in 2002, described the administration. Cleland left the Commission in Decem-

"Oh, for heaven's sake!" Carrington shouted. "He just talked about avoiding partisanship, you left-wing union stooge!"

"Here it comes," Puga sneered. "The Republican congressman steps up to protect the president."

Lyon figured it was best to let the pair fight it out for a bit, and so he sat back and let the shout-fest continue. Former lieutenant governor Beane, seated next to the chairman, raised an eyebrow at Lyon with an expectant look, but the chairman just shrugged.

He leaned over to Beane and whispered, "Running these meetings would be easier if I were armed," triggering giggles in the octogenarian.

JUNE 2007
U.S. National Debt: $8.86 trillion

Months later, the commission's hearings began, with the requisite television coverage. CNN put away the "Drums of War" introduction music, and instead the accelerating, synthesizer-heavy "Emergency Beat" was the musical theme of choice.

"Into the Lyon's den," boomed Wolf Blitzer in a pun used much too frequently this week.

"It is being called the worst mistake in the history of American agricultural policy! Millions of dollars in economic damage as thousands of western farmers battled a herbivorous predator: cheatgrass. With the country's agriculture sector

---

ber 2003 after many other commissioners feared his angry, partisan views about the Bush administration would erode the credibility of their efforts. In a deal quietly arranged by Sen. Tom Daschle, Cleland was appointed to a $136,000-per-year appointment to the Export-Import Bank, a nomination put forth by the very administration he so vehemently opposed. He was replaced by former Nebraska senator Bob Kerrey. Philip Shenon, *The Commission*, pp. 162–163.

just beginning to recover from the invasion, now is the time for hard questions and harder answers," Blitzer said, making a mental note to vigorously shake whoever had loaded up the in-camera teleprompter that day. "Today on Capitol Hill, the National Cheatgrass Disaster Commission aims its crosshairs at Adam Humphrey—the longtime administrative director of the U.S. Department of Agriculture's Agency of Invasive Species."

. . .

For Adam Humphrey, a man who had carefully avoided the public spotlight, the hearing presented a momentous challenge. Sure, his occasional address to agricultural groups had been used as late-night filler for C-SPAN, and he had testified on Capitol Hill at least once a year, but he had never been expected to work his persuasive charms upon a national television audience.

But he had practiced for weeks . . . and he knew he had at least one ally on the panel.

. . .

Congressman Bader's staff had told their boss, repeatedly, that attending the commission hearing would be a bad idea. They had noticed that Bader, usually cool, calm, and cerebral as one of the House's preeminent number-crunching budget hawks, could quickly flip out when discussing the Agency of Invasive Species and particularly Adam Humphrey. The staff figured that Humphrey would spin the facts with the intensity of a wind tunnel, and that the odds of Bader stifling the urge to loudly call out the untruths were nil. Bader's colleague, Congressman Joe Wilson of South Carolina, warned him that if he lost control during an opponent's comments, it would backfire greatly.

So it was arranged that Bader would watch the hearings' live television feed from a small overflow room adjacent to the hearing room, and he had his instant message system connected to the laptop in front of Carrington.

Bader would never think of influencing the proceedings of the bipartisan commission; he merely wanted to make sure he could provide any necessary information to the commission in a timely—instant, really—manner.

. . .

At noon, the hearings began. Humphrey adjusted the microphone before him.

"To the members of this commission, members of Congress, and to the American public, I apologize," Humphrey began. "The performance of this agency was not what the American people have come to expect from us."

He held his fist to his mouth, mugging regret, and he heard the relentless *click-click-click* of the assembled photographers, who had been conditioned to greet any hand gesture by taking a number of photographs appropriate for a UFO landing.

"As we move forward together with the distinguished members of this commission, in unraveling the mysteries of the cheatgrass infestation and the difficulty in harnessing sufficient resources to deal with the menace to our agricultural community, I would urge the distinguished public servants before me to recognize that any thorough review of our actions will reveal that the problem was not a lack of judgment or any individual decision. Instead, I see a serious structural, systemic problem that blocked any of us from taking the necessary action."

. . .

In the overflow room, Bader yelled at the television; his staff hoped he couldn't be heard outside.

"Here it comes," Bader said. "Here's the scapegoat! *It wasn't me! It was the one-armed man!*"

. . .

"As administrative director, it is commonly assumed that my job is to ensure that the agency does everything it needs to do. That assumption is incorrect. To do everything needed would require more staff and more hours in a day than currently exist. Requests for assistance and information come in, by the dozens or hundreds per day, each day, throughout the year. Requests from farmers, gardeners, ranchers, requests from state and local agencies, requests from experts in the field, requests from forestry experts, U.S. Fish and Wildlife Service."

. . .

"Gee, if only we had spent enormous sums building a giant database network to organize all of the requests and data like Weed.gov—oh, that's right! We did!" fumed Bader.

. . .

"Most notable are the requests that we are legally required to respond to in a timely matter—FOIA requests, budgetary requests, and perhaps most significantly, congressional requests."

. . .

"You son of a bitch!" Bader gasped. "You're going to blame us!"

. . .

"Put simply, we and every other agency within the federal government must respond to every congressional request and without delay; to ignore any one of them is to risk being found in contempt of Congress," Humphrey said, pausing to shake his head in regret.

Javier Puga piped up with a line of questioning that seemed all too perfect, almost rehearsed: "Mr. Humphrey, it sounds like you're saying that congressional oversight, designed to ensure efficiency and service to the people, is one of your primary obstacles to achieving efficiency and service to the people."

"Absolutely!" exclaimed Humphrey. "We face severe consequences for failing to respond to a congressional request for information, assistance, or almost any other request; we face significantly lesser consequences for failing to respond to a request from a member of the general public. I wish it were otherwise, the folly of this system has been abundantly clear since my first day at the agency, but to change it, we would need to change the culture of Capitol Hill."

"This is like watching scapegoating jujitsu," Lisa marveled from the audience.

"Undoubtedly, our agency needs to develop a better system of processing information about invasive species," Humphrey continued. "I would prefer a system that included less stove-piping of information through particular channels."

Commissioner Caleb Lyon cleared his throat, and underneath the desk kicked Beane, who had closed his eyes and was not discernibly awake. "Mr. Humphrey, could you please give us a sense of how you envision a system that has less . . . 'stove-piping,' as you describe it?"

"It would be wise to think of these incoming reports of weeds, bugs, and other invasive species as intelligence, not data," Humphrey said. "Data just gets stored somewhere; intelligence is meant to be acted upon," and the septuagenarians and octogenarians on the commission nodded. "Secondly, perhaps we need a separate director whose job would be to focus particularly on which invasive weed species represent immediate threats to our communities."

Puga piped up again: "It sounds like you think your agency would be helped if you had a . . . a director of weed intelligence."

"Indeed, Congressman," Humphrey smiled.

"A DWI," Carrington scoffed.

There was an audible "OW!" from outside the chamber; no one inside the hearing room knew that it was produced by Nick Bader punching a wall and breaking a finger bone.

SEPTEMBER 2007
U.S. National Debt: $9 trillion

The Washington hearing had been of limited use to the commission—the networks cut away as soon as Humphrey began his forty-nine-minute soliloquy about the unpredictable nature of wind patterns on the U.S.-Mexican border. But the field hearing in California was, in retrospect, a mistake.

Lyon felt the commission needed to hear from those most directly impacted by the cheatgrass epidemic, so the members were flown out to Southern California to meet with farmers. He arranged so that the members would travel together as a group—even all going in the same van, driven by the commissioner himself—in an effort to build camaraderie and teamwork.

The morale of the commission had steadily declined from the beginning. Puga and Carrington treated the work as mortal combat, and could barely stand to be in the same room with each other. As commissioners, they were learning to loathe and detest each other in ways that they never had as colleagues in the House. Meanwhile, the pace and duration of the workload began to wear on the Four Fogeys; they were starting to repeat questions, lose focus, and nod off in meetings more regularly. Lyon began to wonder what would happen if one keeled over before the commission finished its work, and how to handle any 3–3 splits in their assessments.

The field hearing in Temecula, California, had started off well enough, with detailed descriptions of how the farmers had dealt with cheatgrass in the past and how and why the 2006 growing season had differed so dramatically. But only twenty minutes passed before one farmer had asked the commissioners about the possibility of a "federal compensation fund," and with that door open, every subsequent witness followed. The cost of the cheatgrass losses described by the witnesses suddenly jumped in comparison to the written testimony submitted before the hearing.

What was scheduled to be a two-hour hearing turned into four and a half hours of farmers explaining why the federal government, or somebody, really owed them several hundred thousand dollars to make up for everything. Lyon entered the hearing with high hopes of encountering "real" Americans—humble, plainspoken, salt-of-the-earth family farmers who would be a refreshing change from the blame-shifting bureaucrats they had interviewed in Washington. Instead, he found the collection of witnesses to be surprisingly high with whiners and grifters.

The air conditioning in the van was weakening, they had made several wrong turns, and the flight back to Washington was a redeye. Puga had complained about the amenities every step of the way, and he seethed that Carrington had upgraded himself. Carrington had remarked that the exorbitant cost of the first-class ticket was worth it, just for the opportunity to remind Puga that he was not permitted to use the first-class bathroom.

"Could you please turn the vents on the air conditioning so that they reach the backseats?" snarled Puga.

Carrington looked like he was adjusting the vents, and perhaps moved them one degree closer to the center, between the front seats.

"The air conditioning is weak, it doesn't matter which way the vents are pointing!" Carrington shot back.

"I wouldn't know, because you've had the center vent pointed at yourself this whole trip!" Puga spat.

"What, are you guys twelve?" groused Lyon, fairly certain he was supposed to make that last turn to get back to the airport; he wondered why all the intersections had NO U TURNS signs.

"I shouldn't be surprised," Puga said. "Just like a spoiled elitist to hog all of the air conditioning for himself!"

"Oh, look, the hothead full of hot air can't take the heat!" sniped Carrington. "I'm so shocked that you're complaining, because it's not like you've spent your entire legal career complaining, and your entire congressional career complaining, and all of your time on this commission complaining!"

"I'm only complaining because of injustices perpetrated by the likes of you and your right-wing friends! If you guys hadn't started all this by—"

"I DON'T CARE WHO STARTED IT, I WILL TURN THIS VAN AROUND RIGHT NOW!" bellowed an irate Lyon. "NOW SHUT UP, THE BOTH OF YOU, FOR THE REST OF THIS TRIP!"

The remainder of the car ride was quiet, except for the snoring of two of the Four Fogeys.

. . .

After the California trip, the draft report came about surprisingly quickly. Even Puga was willing to acknowledge a long litany of missed warnings, lackadaisical response, communications breakdowns between field offices and headquarters, and a general culture of complacency that ensured the agency's response would not meet the challenge of the cheatgrass outbreak.

Puga argued that the solution was additional staffers to "facilitate communications and ensure proper prioritization," while Carrington wanted to clean house as far and wide as possible.

Lyon pushed the two to adopt a multistep process: dismiss the upper management to ensure accountability; bring in new managers to audit the operations to figure out where to cut the fat and ensure the clearest, most direct lines of communication; and then possibly make staff additions based on the needs.

. . .

The receptionist at the commission offices buzzed Lyon, and told him he had a visitor.

It was Humphrey.

Humphrey entered, nodded, and stood before Lyon's desk.

"I am . . . preparing my exit from the agency," Humphrey announced.

13

JANUARY 2008
U.S. National Debt: $9.23 trillion
Budget, USDA Agency of Invasive Species: $279.5 million

Lyon stared back.

"You didn't seem like a man eager to resign at last summer's hearing, Humphrey," he said, gesturing to his guest to take a seat.

"I am not, Mr. Chairman," Humphrey said, sitting. "But a time like this makes one focus one's priorities. I hear the rumors, Mr. Chairman. The word is that you'll be seeking wholesale changes in management, a decision that I fear would be horrific to the operations and effectiveness of the agency I've spent my entire career working in. Thus, if there must be a scapegoat to be sacrificed, let it be me, instead of any of the dedicated career civil servants beneath me."

"*Right,*" said Lyon, incapable of packing more skepticism into a single word.

"Mr. Chairman, I have come to accept that my departure is a foregone conclusion. But I want to do everything to ensure a smooth transition, and I was hoping the commission could assist with that."

"How so?"

"Allow me to begin by asking whether the commission's final report, as currently drafted, calls for my dismissal or resignation."

"Our recommendations are secret until the report is finalized."

Humphrey gave him a skeptical look.

"Don't buy any green bananas," said Lyon.

"I disagree with that, but I understand the conclusion," Humphrey sighed. "If it is all the same to you, with my departure approaching either way, I would urge the commission to . . . omit that."

"Replacing the manager who permitted the agency's performance to reach this piss-poor level is pretty much the heart of our recommendations," Lyon growled.

"A recommendation that is moot if I have one foot out the door," countered Humphrey. "In fact, if I announced my resignation tomorrow, you would be calling for something already done. Suddenly the centerpiece of your recommendations would be moot, making your final report . . . safe. Irrelevant. Some might even dismiss it as predictable and inconsequential, an offering of window dressing from a commission that had so boldly promised true accountability. Now, if I were in your position—"

"You're not."

"I would focus my report on some other recommendation beyond rubber-stamping the replacement of the soon-to-depart administrative director."

Lyon sized up Humphrey, and began to see that the bureaucrat had a point.

"We're also recommending the creation of that DWI position," Lyon said. "Stupid acronym."

"Ah, the director of weed intelligence, now *that* is a groundbreaking reform proposal!" Humphrey replied, offering an approving nod.

"I'm so glad you approve, considering that it was your proposal."

"Indeed, and it represents a fundamental, structural transformation of the management of the agency," Humphrey said, realizing he had accidentally slipped into his Gingrichian buzzwords from the 1990s. "If nothing else, under a new system with one person with a clearly defined responsibility to prevent problems like this one, you know precisely who to turn to if, heaven forbid, this ever happens again."

"Well, when you describe the DWI as a professional on-staff scapegoat, I can't wait." Lyon's sarcasm probably qualified as a weapon of mass destruction. "Explain to me again why we shouldn't call for your ass to be canned immediately."

"Because, if you do, there will be great pressure to get me out as quickly as possible," Humphrey explained matter-of-factly. "When a crisis occurs, there's always a call to have heads roll. Many wanted George Tenet fired on September 12. Could you imagine the mood within the CIA if, at the precise moment they're called to scour the earth for the world's most wanted men, the boss was summarily fired and everyone else within the organization feared for their jobs? What did we want them focused upon, the task at hand or covering their rears?"

"The cheatgrass crisis has long since passed," Lyon said.

"But you and I know that in Washington, another crisis is never far away," Humphrey said. "I am an old man, with retirement in sight even before this mess began. Yes, new leadership is necessary—but don't exacerbate the problems at my agency by throwing in some new administrative director who has to learn on the job."

Lyon gradually nodded.

. . .

Humphrey broke the news to Wilkins in his office.

"You told them you're leaving?" gasped Wilkins. "I mean, I knew this would come someday, but—"

"I said I would leave, but I made no promises on when. The transition is in progress. In some ways, the transition began the day you walked through the door to work with me."

"That was 1979, Adam."

"Some transitions are longer than others," he shrugged. "I'll leave . . . in the next year or so."

Wilkins smirked. "Or so."

"I've done almost everything I wanted to do here," Humphrey said with a satisfied sigh. "With one exception. When I hand the baton to you, I want to do it in the new building."

⋅ ⋅ ⋅

The two men met later that night at the bar at the Willard InterContinental hotel.

"To an illustrious career," Wilkins raised his glass of scotch.

"I'm not gone yet," Humphrey said with a smirk, drinking.

"I'm not even sure that you needed to announce your resignation-date-to-be-named-later maneuver," Wilkins said. "I checked the legislation establishing the commission and found Congress gave it no statutory authority."

"Of course not, that would mean Congress would be giving up some of its power," Humphrey scoffed. "The 9/11 Commission, the Katrina Commission, the Iraq Study Group, the various Social Security and entitlement reform panels, every endlessly touted 'blue ribbon commission'—they're there to tell Congress what it ought to do, but not to enact the recommendations themselves."

"Still, you don't really have to go," Wilkins said, feeling like he could enjoy his imminent accession to Humphrey's job once he had given his boss every opportunity to resist the exit. "Lyon can call for you to be fired until he's blue in the face, but—"

"Reassuring to know my protégé does his legal homework," Humphrey smiled. "I briefly contemplated that path, but why create the headlines of an unnecessary fight to stay on for another year or two? Within forty-eight hours, my name will be out of the headlines, and our illustrious agency will revert to its traditional level of attention, which is to say, none."

"A shame you had to be the scapegoat, Adam," Wilkins said.

"It does seem rather un-American," Humphrey sighed. "When it was discovered that corporations were being given millions of dollars in subsidies to 'promote exports'—run advertising overseas—was anyone put in the public stocks? Pelted with rotten fruit? Was anyone punished when the 1981 federal budget was so hastily and chaotically assembled that the phone number of a staffer that was scribbled on a margin ended up being printed in the final legislation?"

"I never heard that story," Wilkins giggled.

"255-4833," Humphrey replied. "I just wished it had been a few pages later, we could have used another two and a half million in our funding."

"I'll bet with inflation, today it would be $8,675,309!" laughed Wilkins, but Humphrey didn't get the joke. "You see, it's a phone number. In a song. It goes 8-6-7-5—oh, you know, forget it."

"When all of those dedicated citizen-legislators from the 1994 landslide changed their minds on term limits, did anyone complain? Did their constituents rise up in outrage?"

"My new house isn't worth what I paid for it a few years ago!" Wilkins exclaimed. "Anybody losing their jobs over that?"

"No WMDs in Iraq! We're still in Afghanistan! New Orleans is a mess!" Humphrey continued. "Disasters all around! Why does our disaster require heads to roll when so many others continue unabated?"

"Every Middle East envoy is told to go to make peace out there, and they come back empty-handed! CEOs get golden parachutes, actors and directors turn out dreck, the press gets things wrong all the time, nothing works the way it's supposed to, and that's the way it's always been!" shouted an inebriated Wilkins.

"Unaccountability!" the now-tipsy Humphrey roared. "It's the American way!"

OCTOBER 2008
U.S. National Debt: $10.5 trillion

"You're going to lose," Nick Bader's campaign manager said quietly.

"This is the kind of can-do spirit I've come to expect from the most expensive consultants money can buy," Bader responded dryly.

The two sat alone in the district campaign headquarters. It was late, and most of the staffers had gone home.

"We've run the numbers every which way," the manager said with a heavy sigh. "Obama is going to steamroll McCain in your district. The brand is absolutely toxic. People aren't sure exactly why Wall Street is crashing and why all of the financial news keeps depicting a future that looks like *Mad Max*, but they're fairly certain all of this is your fault."

"I can't believe it," Bader said, looking at a television that featured one attack ad after another during the commercial breaks. One from Obama ended, followed by one from Bader's Democratic rival, depicting Bader morphing into Ebenezer Scrooge.

"How can our messaging be this weak?" exclaimed Bader. "What about the ads that are supposed to hammer him on raising income taxes, raising the inheritance tax, or—?"

"A big chunk of the voters in this district don't pay any income tax," the campaign manager shrugged. "They don't have much to inherit, or much to leave their kids after the market tanked. All of your talk on taxes seems very alien to them, very far from what's worrying them right now."

Bader watched the caricature of himself as a Dickensian miser get picked up by a small crowd of people and get tossed off a cliff. Bader's smooth-talking rival appeared, in a crisp blue shirt with the sleeves rolled up. Bader was fairly certain he had made a similar ad back when he first ran in 1994.

"For too long, men like Nick Bader have kept our public finances in a straitjacket, leaving core needs dangerously unfunded," the rival said. "For decades, a dangerous, right-wing, antigovernment ideology has run roughshod over Washington, cutting spending to the bone and leaving millions of Americans hurting. For far too long, we've let them argue that government can and should do less. But we know, in our hearts, and in our souls, government can and must do more."

14

MARCH 2009

U.S. National Debt: $11.23 trillion

Budget, USDA Agency of Invasive Species: $340.06 million

The Washington Post

Style Section, page C1   April 3, 2009

D.C.'s Unsung Heroes No More:
The New Dashing Bureaucrats

By Siobhan Nivens, Washington Post Staff Writer

For decades, the cliché of choice among those who disdain government has been to dismiss its employees as mere "bureaucrats."

But bold, outspoken figures have refuted that tired notion in recent years.

The faceless government employees are no longer so faceless, and the American public is seeing that the government workers who keep the wheels of government turning are brave, righteous, dashing—and yes, even stylish.

FBI special agent Coleen Rowley, who excoriated her agency for missteps in catching terrorists before 9/11, was named one of *Time* magazine's Newsmakers of the Year.

In 2004, Richard Clarke, the White House's National Coordinator for Security, Infrastructure Protection and Counterterrorism, heroically wrote a book about how no one listened to him.

Now, shortly after the election of a president who thoroughly defended the necessity and effectiveness of the federal government in the daily lives of Americans, there is a new iconoclast to add to that list: Adam Humphrey, the administrative director for the U.S. Department of Agriculture's Agency of Invasive Species—soon to retire from government service after thirty years.

The Agency of Invasive Species was created almost as an afterthought after Jimmy Carter encountered a weed infestation on his peanut farm in 1974. Launched as a small office within the U.S. Department of Agriculture in 1977, it became a separate agency in 1978, and Humphrey began as the agency's first—and until quite recently, only—administrative director. His longtime deputy, Jack Wilkins, will take over sometime in the coming months.

"A lot of the attention in Washington goes to those who come and go," Humphrey says in his office. "The talking heads, this rising star on the Hill, presidents and so on. The true unsung heroes of Washington—the ones whom the Republic would quickly collapse without—are the vast armies of largely unknown, diligent federal workers, keeping their heads down and making sure that everything works as it should."

As an administrative director, Humphrey found himself at the forefront of Washington's budget battles over the past decades, a fight he feels represents an existential one for the kind of America he and his fellow federal workers envision.

"It seems a never-ending battle, with our budgetary existence forever on the precipice," Humphrey says. "It's always tossed around so willy-nilly, this talk of 'cut spending!' and 'oh, cut this, cut that,' but so few really stop to examine the real-world consequences of those bland lines of zeroes on the balance sheets." He pauses, gazing out at the cramped cubicles outside his office. "All too many among the cut-government crowd don't understand that what we do isn't about politics. It's about people."

The Agency of Invasive Species toiled in relative obscurity for most of its existence, until a cheatgrass weed infestation in 2006 caused enormous crop losses in California.

The agricultural crisis generated headlines and screams that the agency had dropped the ball and failed in its mission. More than a few voices on Capitol Hill blamed Humphrey, and several lawmakers, including former Rep. Nicholas Bader, R-Penn., called for his resignation.

"Dark days indeed," Humphrey says. "Of course, Congressman Bader had been calling for my resignation every year since he arrived in 1995." (Bader did not return a request for comment for this article.)

But Humphrey artfully dodged the slings and arrows of the right-wing critics, and ultimately a bipartisan commission concluded that the agency's response to the weed outbreak was hindered by "systemic failures."

Now the agency will soon be moving into newer state-of-the-art offices, settling into a particularly envied patch of Washington real estate.

The construction site just southeast of the Washington Monument has generated its share of grumbling from architecture critics, and more than a few Washingtonians have wondered why a relatively small agency should get such a prominent space.

"First, we need to be close to the rest of the Department of Agriculture, just down the street. And the claim that the architecture is ostentatious is simply ridiculous. Look at the Patent and Trademark Office in Alexandria," Humphrey says. "It's

CONTINUED ON PAGE C8

The Washington Post

Outlook Section, Page D1   April 17, 2009

The Runaway Agency: A Primer on Washington Gone Wrong

By Ava Summers

A recent *Washington Post* Style section article by Siobhan Nivens profiled Adam Humphrey, the soon-to-depart administrative director for the U.S. Department of Agriculture's Agency of Invasive Species, in laudatory terms.

From 1993 to 1999, I worked as a systems analyst at the AIS, and returned there as a contractor from 2001 to 2006 before departing to write about the relationship between government and technology for *Wired* and other publications.

Far from a role model for other managers in the public sector, Adam Humphrey is perhaps better described as the personification of all that is wrong with the federal government's workforce.

Budget data show that the budget for the Agency of Invasive Species grew at four times the rate of inflation from 1977 to 2009. During this time, data compiled by the agency—a not entirely reliable source—indicate that the number of responses to invasive species infestations grew at less than half that pace. While the number of agency employees is maddeningly difficult to ascertain from public records, it is safe to conclude that the number of employees under Humphrey across the country also increased by a rate much greater than inflation. And then, of course, the agency had its most prominent failure during the cheatgrass crisis of 2006.

A lot more money, and a lot more employees, yielded only a modest increase in action during Humphrey's tenure, climaxing with a catastrophic failure four years ago. Despite a pledge during subsequent hearings that he would resign, Humphrey has hung around for three years.

The agency doesn't fail every day; it succeeds often enough, toiling in an obscure manner on a topic most Americans ignore. But it is spin to argue that it generates anything more than mediocrity at best, offering abysmal value, with little inclination to improve its performance. Humphrey didn't deserve a 2,000-word send-off with a glamorous photo; his career deserved a dissection of how the federal government can defenestrate his mentality from its ranks.

This is not the complaint of a bitter former employee; both of my departures from AIS were voluntary.

If you read publications like *Government Executive* and talk to anyone in human resources, they will tell you that the federal government needs young workers, that it covets their energy, their drive, their enthusiasm.

This is all a pack of lies.

If a young worker has the patience to go through the Byzantine hiring process, they get the signal, early on, that no one is really interested in utilizing their energy, their drive, their enthusiasm. Oftentimes those traits will be perceived as a silly waste of time or an annoyance. At far too many federal offices, a culture of complacency took root years or decades ago, and shows no sign of lifting. Most offices have well-established routines and have no interest in disrupting them.

And then there is the incompetence. Most federal managers are terrified of firing workers—fear of lawsuits, fear of confrontation, fear of workplace violence. The "Peter Principle" may be universal, but in the federal government, the least competent workers are often reassigned and shuffled around.

When competent workers see the incompetent among them hanging around with no repercussions for repeated failure— often enjoying a lighter workload, since no one trusts them with any task of any consequence—it is a corrosive acid to their drive, diligence, professionalism, and pride. The message is clear: No one really cares how well you do your job. Just punch in, keep your head down, and punch out.

It doesn't help that promotions and raises are often allocated based on seniority, instead of actual performance or innovation.

These problems are worse in some federal offices than others, but pervasive enough to be a national problem, and one that receives astonishingly little attention from the so-called "serious" thinkers in the public policy world. The American people's skepticism and criticism of government is not some result of a propagandizing effect of talk radio, Fox News, or blogs. It is the result of decades of interacting with federal workers and finding the quality of service rendered to be way less than the increasingly expensive cost.

Public skepticism and derision is fueled by unresponsive offices and their incomprehensible voice mail trees, by regulations written and enforced by those who will never have to follow them, by allegations of Minerals Management Service staff partying with the companies they were supposed to be regulating, by the unprofessional wandering hands of TSA workers, by sleeping air traffic controllers, and by the revelation that tens of thousands of federal workers owe billions in back taxes. Each new scandal—grabbing headlines for a few days, then fading away—paints a vivid and more detailed culture of waste, inefficiency, and an entitled, even spoiled view of the public treasury.

I hope that there is a greater culture of accountability and focus on results in places like the Central Intelligence Agency and Federal Bureau of Investigation, with life-and-death consequences to their duties, than I saw at the AIS under Adam Humphrey. My sense is that there is, as well as in other corners of the federal government where complacency or incompetence can have lethal results: the Centers for Disease Control, the National Transportation Safety Board, the Food and Drug Administration, the military. But changing the culture of the non-life-and-death jobs within the federal government requires a president, a cabinet, a Congress, and indeed a public that demands much better than what they've been getting for a very long time.

Ava Summers covers government and technology issues for Wired.

15

MAY 2009

U.S. National Debt: $11.3 trillion

Budget, USDA Agency of Invasive Species: $340.06 million

Ava's second stint at the Agency of Invasive Species, attempting to get a clunky information technology system to come somewhere close to meeting the organization's needs, was less dramatic but only marginally less satisfying than her first one. After a few years of trying to get folks to understand the basics of network security, she felt that same rising tide of frustration within her.

"I can't stand this place, I need an outlet," she lamented one afternoon to Lisa.

"Take up Pilates," Lisa offered.

Ava shook her head. "No, I mean, if I waste any more of my life in one more time-sucking meeting, I'm going to try to electrocute myself with the nearest outlet."

Ava began writing up short descriptions of the complications of getting the government to use the Web efficiently; on various tech-head Web chat boards, she built a following as a tart-tongued critic of the way the government did its business, once labeling it "a giant glob of cholesterol clogging the arteries of Americans' inherent dynamism." All around her she saw the

Internet revolution that had once excited her—smartphones, Twitter, Facebook, ubiquitous scanners, downloaders, texters, signals, bandwidth—and yet daily life within the halls of the government changed slowly, when it changed it all.

Her online explanations of the war between the bureaucratic mentality and the rapidly changing world outside the bureaucracy's walls led to occasional freelance pieces. Eventually, she joined the staff of *Wired* as she rapidly became the recipient of every "You think *your* office is screwed up? Wait until you hear about mine!" missive from across the federal bureaucracy coast to coast.

Now residing in Arlington, Ava still saw Lisa and Jamie, but less frequently. Lisa was putting in the long hours, angling for the deputy executive director position. Apparently Wilkins had made clear that he liked her and trusted her from their years of working together during the cheatgrass crisis, but he had to make sure that any outside review of the long and complicated hiring process would give no indication that he had hired a longtime associate that he liked and trusted from years of working together.

Jamie and her Marine husband became parents, and Ava found her old friend . . . content, but kind of boring. The light from that luminous vision she had described two decades earlier, of planning grand international summits, dimmed a little more each day. Life became more focused on her son, and the house in the outer suburbs, and balancing the schedule of her event planning for the agency, and her husband's work as a defense contractor.

. . .

Ever since he had read her piece in the Sunday Outlook section of the *Post*, former Congressman Nick Bader had been trying to get in touch with Ava Summers. Finally she agreed to have lunch at the America! restaurant in Union Station; she concluded if he was so insistent to meet, she could at least get a good meal out of it.

"Your op-ed was great," Bader wiped a bit of food from his chin. "I think it had people choking on their Cheerios all over the *Washington Post*'s circulation area. It said a lot of things that needed to be said, a lot of things that people in this city just walk by, oblivious to, ignoring, averting their eyes, pretending everything's fine. I saw it early on, and tried to . . . well, I mean, even back when I was working for Reagan, we were supposed to be cutting the bureaucracy. And then with Newt. And then with Bush."

Ava nodded. "I remember when I worked at AIS, people talked about you as if you were some combination of Timothy McVeigh and Mephistopheles."

"Really?" Bader emitted a grim chuckle. "You know, for all of that, you would think I had actually managed to cut a budget or two. No, I, uh . . . I was . . . there was something Sisyphean in my efforts, over a lot of years in Congress. It's not getting beat after seven terms that hurts, it's the sense that I could have and should have done more in those seven terms that keeps me up at night."

Ava was slightly unnerved by the intensity of the regret in Bader's eyes.

"You know, this lunch is nice, if you just wanted to say you liked my piece, you could have just sent an e-mail."

"I have a . . . proposition for you," Bader said uneasily. "Adam Humphrey's crowning achievement is that monstrosity they're building next to the Washington Monument."

"I know," she sighed. "This guy I'm dating gripes about it; he says they took away a perfectly good flag football field on that spot."

"Ava, I've had some information brought to me that could allow you and I to . . . make sure it never opens."

Ava stared at him, wondering just how insane the man in front of her really was.

"Congressman, please don't tell me you're working with domestic terrorists."

"What? No!" he exclaimed. "No, no, I'd never do something like that. Jesus! How could you think that—look, never mind. The bottom line is, there are a lot of ways to delay a construction project."

"Go on."

"One of my old committee staffers got a tour of the construction site with a congressional delegation two weeks ago. They're going through this state-of-the-art, no expense spared, federal office building of the future, blah blah blah. But then he says, as they're walking through the top floor, he says he saw a couple of bags of drywall with Chinese writing on it."

Ava stared blankly. "What, did that violate some 'Buy American' law or something?"

"At the very least!" howled Bader. "How much have you heard about Chinese drywall?"

"I rent, I don't worry about HGTV stuff," she replied.

Bader explained that defective drywall had been made in China and imported to the U.S. for about a decade, and that the stuff could emit various noxious gases, including hydrogen sulfide, creating a stink and other human health issues. In addition, the gases could tarnish and damage copper pipes, wiring, air conditioner coils, and some types of jewelry.

"What's more, last year the EPA found some types of drywall were particularly vulnerable to a mold that originated in Southeast Asia," he continued, consulting a pile of papers from a folder he brought in his briefcase. "Something where the mold grows at faster rates, spews spores, aggravates asthma and re-spiratory problems—your basic health and lawsuit nightmare."

Ava chuckled. "Gee, somebody should get the Agency of In-vasive Species right on that."

"I know, right?" he said, eyes bulging. "Here's the problem. If I or this staffer go to the EPA, and say, hey, we saw some-thing . . . there's no guarantee they'll take it seriously. I'm on record as saying the building is a disaster, my opinions on how that agency should be eliminated are well known, and appar-ently some blogs are spreading the rumor that I'm obsessed and unhinged!"

"I can't imagine why," Ava tried really, really hard to not sound sarcastic.

"Anyway, if we want the EPA or General Services Admin-istration to take this seriously, we need evidence. And the AIS isn't just going to hand it over."

Ava wondered when Bader had become so comfortable with the pronoun "we," and she had a feeling Bader's idea was going to get very complicated.

. . .

Ava thought that Bader's plan was particularly insane—perhaps losing office had left him seeing conspiracies all around him, or devising elaborate plans of action to right a wrong turn of political history—and so her first step was to try a much sim-pler approach.

She called Lisa.

"I didn't expect to hear from you," Lisa greeted her rather icily.

"Yes, I know, we haven't talked in a while, and I'm sorry. But something big has come up, and it involves your job."

"What?" Lisa said, with a hostility that Ava didn't seem to pick up on.

"So, if I heard the new office building you're supposed to move into next year was a public health hazard, you would want me to do something about it, right?"

Lisa dropped her hostility for a moment. *"What?"*

Ava repeated the question.

"That . . . question was in English, but the words make no sense in the order you put them."

"I heard a rumor that they used Chinese drywall in the building."

"Well, I mean, how seriously do you take the rumor?" Lisa asked. "I spend my days knocking down all kinds of nonsense rumors."

"Let's say, serious enough. If I told, say, Wilkins, do you think he would take it seriously?"

"Well, Ava, you're not exactly a popular person in the office right now," Lisa said, letting a bit of festering anger flare. "After all, it is spin to argue we *'generate anything more than mediocrity at best, offering abysmal value, with little inclination to improve our performance.'*"

Ava cringed, having momentarily forgotten how her friend would greet the high-profile denunciation of her employer and life's work.

"I'm sorry. Lisa, you know that no matter how much that place drove me nuts, I always thought you were the best. In everything."

"Ava, you trashed my work!" Lisa fumed. "It was harsh, it was demeaning, it was insulting, it was . . . it was . . ."

"All true?" suggested Ava.

"That's beside the point," Lisa said. "I mean, yes, we're a very bureaucratic institution, and yes, this place could drive Mother Teresa into a swearing rage, but it still—"

"Listen, we should talk about this in detail, face to face, sometime soon. But right now I'm sort of in a pressing situation. Do you think I would need evidence to persuade Wilkins or whoever that the new building is a health hazard?"

Long pause on the other end. "Ava, what do you mean, 'evidence'?"

"Someone else I'm dealing with is . . . very determined to go in and check the drywall."

Lisa's pause was long enough where Ava wondered if her cell carrier had dropped the call.

"When you say 'go in and check,' I'm getting a distinct 'break and enter' vibe."

"Your vibe assessment skills have not dulled with age," admitted Ava.

"Have you lost your mind?"

"I'm sorry, Lisa, I don't know if I trust the usual channels on this. If there's a health hazard in there, it would stop the construction, and a lot of people will want to sweep it under the rug."

"You sound like a conspiracy theorist."

"Well, call me crazy for thinking that Humphrey and Wilkins might ignore something that could delay opening up their precious new office!"

Lisa was quiet again, and Ava found that this time her carrier had indeed dropped the call.

. . .

That night, after dark, Ava found herself standing with a former congressman outside a construction site as he walked the perimeter, a leather satchel full of tools, determining the easiest way to sneak into the site.

"What if you're caught?"

"I thought this was a 'we' project," Bader grumbled, examining a chain-link fence gate and concluding that the years of fundraising dinners had made squeezing between them a physical impossibility. "This will be real simple. Get in, get to where my old staffer said he saw the bag, take the samples, get out. Piece of cake. Security is minimal."

"This is breaking and entering a federal facility!" Ava whispered. "This is the sort of thing they send people to Gitmo for!"

"Oh, they'll have Gitmo closed any day now, I'm sure," Bader said. "You coming or not?"

After waiting for a moment, Bader shrugged, and started to climb over the chain-link fence.

Ava watched him, shook her head, and pictured the cover story she would write on the insane ex-Congressman who broke into a construction site to blow open a giant Chinese drywall scandal.

"Wait for me!"

. . .

"If I wasn't so terrified of being arrested, I'd be screaming at you for your insanity," Ava whispered. "You never said we had to go up to the fifth floor!"

Their night had presented only one hitch so far, when Bader awkwardly cleared the chain-link fence and didn't stick the landing, tumbling on his butt in a puddle. Other than the embarrassing stain on the seat of his pants, he had managed to navigate the construction site with a penlight, and he and Ava ascended ten half-flights of railing-free concrete stairs, navigating concrete pillars, piles of rebar, and plastic orange fencing.

From this height, they could see the trailer office by the vehicle entrance to the construction site, and the faint flicker of light within.

"If that guard comes out and sees your flashlight or hears us, we're screwed!"

"He's watching the Nationals," Bader said confidently, even though he was only guessing. "Hope it's a good game and he's focused on that."

In several spots on the fifth floor, Bader had removed a chisel and scraped plaster from unobtrusive corners of the drywall, near the floor and ceiling. He deposited the plaster granules in between two thick sheets of paper and put the material in a small Ziploc bag, labeling each bag's source location with a permanent marker.

"Okay, almost done," Bader whispered, and Ava exhaled. But only for a second.

"I . . . AM . . . SPEECHLESS!" a familiar voice boomed behind them.

Bader and Ava swirled, caught in the glare of another pair of flashlights. They squinted as two figures approached: Adam Humphrey and Jack Wilkins.

Lisa told them, Ava realized.

"What the hell are you doing here?" Bader demanded, in a tone of indignation that was entirely inappropriate for someone who had just hopped a fence and trespassed on federal property.

"I was just about to ask you that, you lunatic. And you, Ms. Summers—what, the op-ed smear wasn't enough?"

"Everything I wrote was true, Humphrey," Ava responded defiantly.

"There's Chinese drywall on this site, Humphrey," Bader said.

"Preposterous, Mr. Bader," Humphrey said firmly. "Your obsessive vendetta against me has driven you mad."

"I am not obsessed!" barked Bader.

"Well, you kinda are," Ava said beside him. "But that doesn't necessarily mean you're wrong. This is worth checking out, guys. If Bader's right, there could be serious health issues for people who work here down the road."

"Do you believe these two?" Humphrey asked Wilkins. "Breaking and entering out of sheer concern for our coworkers, after sneering about them for years. This facility is being made of only the finest materials by the finest construction crew, held to the highest standards—"

"HA!" scoffed Bader.

"You're going to work in this building, Wilkins," Ava warned. "Really want to gamble with your health, and that of all of your coworkers? Hundreds, maybe thousands of people eventually?"

"This is paranoid, conspiratorial nonsense," Humphrey declared, attempting to cut off any doubt on Wilkins's part.

"Adam, why didn't we check in with the guard when we came in?" Wilkins asked.

"Maybe he didn't want the guards knowing they might be exposing themselves to toxic drywall," Bader said, holding up the plastic bags. "You may not care, because you're heading off to your fat pension, but the EPA is going to care. They're going to care enough to stop construction immediately—and then God knows when it gets started again."

Wilkins's jaw dropped in disbelief. "I feel like I'm surrounded by crazy people."

"There's only one crazy person up here, Jack, and he's the one waving around plastic bags full of drywall, rambling that they're tainted with the Andromeda Strain or some such nonsense!" Humphrey shouted.

"What if he's right?" Ava asked.

"What if he's wrong?" Wilkins retorted.

"Mr. Bader, I insist you give me that bag right now!" Humphrey said emphatically.

"Like hell I'm doing that."

Humphrey stepped closer.

"You want it?" Bader said with a certain glee. He backed away a few steps toward a pile of construction supplies, and picked up a three-foot-long piece of rebar, a grooved steel rod that looked positively alien in his soft, wrinkled, pale hand.

Humphrey couldn't stifle a giggle. "You must be joking."

"Come and take it!" Nick Bader was convinced that he looked as daring and strong as King Leonidas at that moment . . . but he didn't.

"Do not threaten me," Humphrey said, awkwardly shifting to a hunched-over posture, his notion of a combat stance. He waved his flashlight around and found another span of rebar, this one about five feet long, and grabbed his own. He picked it up and realized he had absolutely no idea how to use it as a weapon, other than simply swinging it at his target as hard as possible. The heavy metal staff was almost too long to be of any use.

Wilkins and Ava stared, jaws agape. "Uh, guys, before we do anything we regret—" Wilkins stammered.

Bader hadn't expected Humphrey to actually rise to the dare, and now he had his long-hated rival almost begging to raise their conflict to physical combat. His eyes widened as he realized that maybe God was going to make up for all those injustices over the decades by giving him the opportunity to knock the stuffing out of Adam Humphrey.

The pair circled each other, staring, sweating, in disbelief of the sudden potential—even likelihood—of violence before them.

Bader realized the last time he was in a physical altercation was in his teen years. Humphrey nervously shifted his grip on the bar, trying to figure out whether it was better to grip it overhand or underhand or chest level or eye level or OHMYGODHE'SCOMINGTOWARDME!

Humphrey yelped as Bader's body suddenly surged forward; unbeknownst to him, Bader was actually stumbling from a surge of adrenalin coursing through fifty-nine-year-old muscles and mildly arthritic knees. Bader's bar CLANGED against Humphrey's, sending a reverberating shockwave through Humphrey's arms.

Humphrey's terrified yelp gradually turned almost primally aggressive, meaning it dropped one octave until he ran out of air. "YEAARR—AAAAAAAAR–ARR–AAAAAAAAAAAAAAR–ARGH!"

Bader tumbled to one knee but rose quickly, and Humphrey's face registered a sweet, surprised delight that he wasn't dead or even hurt much at all, turning to indignation that Bader had attacked him (as far as he knew). He pushed his bar against Bader's with another loud CLANG ringing through the night air.

"ARGH!"

"ARGH YOU!"

"RARGH!"

Bader flung the plastic bag toward Ava, and began swinging his rebar, offering what he was certain would appear to be a demonstration of elaborate swordsmanship. In fact, Bader looked more like he was having an aneurism or acting out the "Y-M-C-A" dance.

Ava stared at two retirement-age men, tentatively thrusting or swinging pieces of rebar at each other, both secretly terrified of actually hurting the other but also refusing to back down.

"I would say I need a drink, but what I'm seeing makes me doubt my sobriety as is," she muttered.

She reached down for the plastic bag and found . . . Wilkins was holding the other end.

"Ava . . . you can't do this," he said firmly.

Her face hardened, and she yanked the bag away.

"Why not?"

She turned, wondering if all of the men up here were going insane in the night air, and started walking away briskly. Wilkins followed alongside, not quite threatening . . . but not friendly, either.

Through the open spaces in the walls, she could see the Department of Agriculture building. "I spent way too much of my career in that building fighting paperwork and reviews!" she told Wilkins angrily. "This time you guys can get to fight the bureaucracy."

"You drop that on the EPA's desk, it'll louse up everything!" Wilkins shouted. "They'll want to test every corner of this place, and God knows when this building will ever get finished!"

"Good!" Ava shouted. "Red tape, bureaucratic delays, lawyers—now it's all your problem!"

She jabbed a finger in his chest. "You can watch your dream get tied down like Gulliver by a thousand little . . ." She couldn't remember what the little people in *Gulliver's Travels* were called. "Little . . ."

"Lilliputians?" Wilkins offered.

"Yes, those little guys, thank you," she said quickly.

Wilkins glowered.

"All this time—long before you came along—I was Humphrey's prize pupil . . . his protégé. He taught me everything I know about how the system worked—and how it didn't—and how to navigate it, use it, steer it . . . And now I see you're worse than any of us ever were, because you're willing to wreck it all because you never felt appreciated."

Ava bristled.

"Here I am . . . thinking I know how to get things done . . . and now I am helpless, as you take the capstone of my career and tie it up in knots of red tape for . . . years probably."

Wilkins shook his head. He held up his hands in a surrendering pose.

"Well done, Ava. Well done. I mean it when I say, neither Adam Humphrey nor I could have used red tape to louse things up on anywhere near the scale you're about to!"

Now it was Ava's turn to shudder. She looked at the sample bag in her hand.

"All of this," Wilkins motioned around, "is going to stand around, unused, a monument to you. Ava Summers—that bright-eyed, cheery, idealistic chick in fishnets who walked into our office, going on about how she and these computers were going to change the world . . . well, she grew up to be Washington's most petty vendetta artist. You never changed the world, Ava. The world changed you."

She closed her eyes for a moment. She opened them upon the noise of Humphrey and Bader emerging from around the corner, each one with one ugly bump on the head and bloody knuckles. Their direct combat appeared to have ceased once they actually hurt each other.

"You were the idiot who picked up the steel bar!" Humphrey complained. "I could have told you they hurt!"

"What the hell are you doing up here trying to stop me anyway? You're a bureaucrat, not a cop," Bader snapped. They looked down the hallway at Wilkins and Ava, and the bruised Bader immediately smiled upon seeing she still held the plastic bag.

"That's my girl!" he said, pointing, and jutting his chin at Humphrey beside him. "With the samples in that bag, we get the last laugh!"

She continued to look at them, and the bag.

"Congressman, that's not what either of us came to Washington to do," she said firmly. "Not like this."

She tossed the bag through the opening in the scaffolding, and it plummeted out into the abyss.

Bader looked on in horror.

Wilkins looked on, genuinely surprised, and exhaling a bit of relief.

Humphrey stared, trying to understand why she had thrown away her advantage.

. . .

The private security contractor found the quartet when they emerged from the stairwell on the bottom floor.

"I have a key to the site. I, uh, left my wallet when we were touring the site the other day," Wilkins explained, holding up his wallet. "I'm so embarrassed, officer, I'm so sorry."

"All four of you are here to look for a wallet?" the guard asked skeptically.

Bader and Humphrey instinctively threw arms around each others' backs. "We're a close-knit group of friends."

Frowning skeptically, but not eager to begin a round of paperwork, the guard escorted them to the gate and told them to come back during regular hours next time.

. . .

A half block away, when the quartet was sure the guard had returned his attention to the Nationals game, Bader turned to Ava in fury.

"WHAT THE HELL IS WRONG WITH YOU?" he screamed. Wilkins and Humphrey shrugged and walked back toward their cars.

"There are . . . other ways to go about this," she said quietly.

NOVEMBER 2010

U.S. National Debt: $13.8 trillion

Budget, USDA Agency of Invasive Species: $417.88 million

Gil Hasenkamp, the man who defeated seven-term representative Nick Bader in 2008, found this governing thing a lot harder than he expected.

It started with a contentious interview on Fox News early in his term, when the new congressman angrily defended the newly passed stimulus. He insisted, "You can go to Recovery .gov and you can see that not a [*bleep*]-damn dime of stimulus funds was wasted! Everything's right there, even right-wing fools like you can see that!"

Several days later, news organizations noted that the data on Recovery.gov indicated hundreds of thousands of dollars in projects had been allocated to Arizona's 15th Congressional District, Connecticut's 42nd Congressional District, Delaware's 35th Congressional District, and California's 91st Congressional District . . . none of which actually existed. The money was real, but the districts were not, indicating that lax standards for reporting the use of the stimulus funds had rendered the site useless, riddled with bad data.

Then as the Obamacare legislation was discussed and passed, Hasenkamp found his constituents oddly . . . hostile. Every time he assured the crowds at town hall meetings he had read "almost all" of the five thousand pages of legislative text, he found himself shouted down by jeers and boos. Afterward, he told some malcontent with a pocket video recorder that the word he would use to describe the crowd was "revolting"; and within forty-eight hours, it had more than 75,000 views on YouTube.

"He's right, we are in revolt!" declared the red-clad sparkplug running the local Tea Party, Kristi Womack. She had been a district office director for Bader, and it took about three minutes of persuasion to convince her to run for the office of her old boss.

The district race was shifted from "toss-up" to "likely Republican" when Hasenkamp characterized Womack as "some loon always whining about what the Constitution says."

Bader tapped his extensive fundraising network to assist Womack, and was a regular speaker at Tea Party rallies in the district. And Bader had felt that nagging frustration abate a bit, at least since the day his Google search alert pinged with many, many references to "Agency of Invasive Species."

MARCH 2011
U.S. National Debt: $14.2 trillion
Budget, USDA Agency of Invasive Species: $430.12 million

When the Tea Party–backed Republicans took over the House of Representatives, they found themselves almost immediately in public relations combat with the Obama administration about a plethora of issues: a showdown over the debt ceiling, a controversial gun export program called Fast and Furious, efforts to repeal the recently passed health care bill, and so on.

So most of America failed to notice when the House Oversight and Government Reform Committee held hearings about an alleged cover-up of health hazards in a new federal office building. However, the investigation did generate one memorable exchange, which received national attention when it was featured on Jon Stewart's *The Daily Show.*

CHAIRMAN DARRELL ISSA, R-CALIFORNIA: Mr. Wilkins, this committee has copies of communications from

House Committee on Agriculture staffer Michael Sung, former Congressman Nicholas Bader, and former Agency of Invasive Species employee Ava Summers indicating their concerns that Chinese drywall was used in the construction of the new headquarters building at 1500 Independence Avenue Southwest. What did you do in response to those communications?

AGENCY OF INVASIVE SPECIES ADMINISTRATIVE DIRECTOR JACK WILKINS: (inaudible)

ISSA: Mr. Wilkins, please speak up.

WILKINS: Mr. Chairman, on the advice of my counsel, I respectfully decline to answer based upon my Fifth Amendment constitutional privileges.

ISSA: Did you notify the Environmental Protection Agency, the General Services Administration, or any other authority in response to that?

WILKINS: Mr. Chairman, on the advice of my counsel, I again respectfully decline to answer based upon my Fifth Amendment constitutional privileges.

ISSA: Let the record show this committee has found no record of any reply by you or your office to any of their communications. Mr. Wilkins, are you aware that the federal government spent $250 million to build this new building?

WILKINS: On the advice of my counsel, I respectfully decline to answer based upon my Fifth Amendment constitutional privileges.

ISSA: And that instead of moving in next month, as planned, the use of that building is now postponed indefinitely while inspections are made? Mr. Wilkins, are you aware of how many potential lawsuits the federal government will face as a result of your inaction on this?

WILKINS: On the advice of my counsel, I respectfully decline to answer based upon my Fifth Amendment constitutional privileges.

ISSA: I'd like to turn my attention to your predecessor, former administrative director Adam Humphrey, who is also here today, kindly responding to our subpoena.

AGENCY OF INVASIVE SPECIES ADMINISTRATIVE DIRECTOR ADAM HUMPHREY: On the advice of my counsel, I respectfully decline to answer based upon my Fifth Amendment constitutional privileges.

"WHAT IS WRONG WITH THESE PEOPLE?" exclaimed Jon Stewart in mock incredulity. "Answer something! What is the weather outside? What is two plus two? Coke or Pepsi? Who was the better Darren on *Bewitched*? COME ON! GIVE US SOMETHING TO WORK WITH!"

. . .

The House hearings had turned Humphrey and Wilkins into widely mocked poster boys of government incompetence, and anyone who bothered to follow the story knew it had grown out of Ava's widely read *Wired* story, depicting how no one had replied to e-mailed and written warnings about the drywall for an entire year.

The story had begun with a dramatic description of Nicholas Bader climbing over the chain-link fence, explaining that the quirky former congressman had been obsessed with his former staffer's claim of seeing Chinese drywall on the building site.

But the heart of the story was that Bader, his former staffer, and Ava ultimately went through the "proper channels," communicating their concerns about a health risk to workers in the building. Ava saw this as giving Wilkins one more chance to prove that the agency could overcome its bureaucratic inertia under his management. When a year passed, with no indication that anyone in the government had done anything, then she publicized the concerns, leading to the hearings.

The day after the *Daily Show* segment, Ava went to her front door to find a flower delivery. It was from Nicholas Bader, now on the board of a nonprofit activist group fighting for spending cuts, the Foundation for a Less Expensive America (FLEA).

She looked at the note.

> Dammit, Ava, when you fight, you slice like a hammer! Keep up the good fight!
>
> Nick

She smiled and returned to work on the inevitable follow-up; unfortunately, she was second to the story.

USAD OFFICIAL TO RESIGN

The director of the Department of Agriculture's Agency of Invasive Species has resigned after revelations that his office ignored warnings about the use of dangerous toxic drywall in the construction of a new headquarters building in Washington.

Jack Wilkins, 56, had been with the agency since 1979 and had run the agency since 2009.

It was, the EPA found, a very small amount of substandard drywall; a subcontractor to a subcontractor supplying the drywall had a theft shortly before shipment to the AIS building site, and replaced the missing material from another source.

The process of determining it all, however, delayed the opening of the building until Thanksgiving 2012.

NOVEMBER 2012
U.S. National Debt: $16.3 trillion
Budget, USDA Agency of Invasive Species: $493.58 million

Vice President Joe Biden was the guest of honor for the ribbon-cutting ceremony of the new Vernon Hargis Agency of Invasive Species Building at 1500 Independence Avenue Southwest.

The vice president, giddy over his reelection earlier in the month, only made brief remarks; the highlight was undoubtedly his declaration that "I'm glad you people are on the job, because I [inaudible] can't stand weeds," although some disputed whether the inaudible comment was really all that inaudible, and some wondered whether the vice president's subsequent comparison of invasive species to hemorrhoids in his off-text remarks really fit the tone of the occasion.

Adam Humphrey, now sixty-seven, attended, and the vice president was supposed to thank him in his remarks but called him "Appleby" instead.

After the ceremonies and good-byes were done, Humphrey strolled up 15th Street, past the Washington Monument, and around the Ellipse, taking a look at the White House.

Looking through the fence, he heard a familiar voice behind him.

"You must be quite proud of your victory," Nick Bader said.

"I was about to say the same to you," Humphrey said, only mildly surprised to see his old nemesis. "You drove out Wilkins."

"He's retiring with a full pension. Just like you. Your agency's budget is bigger than ever."

"I never got a chance to work in that beautiful new building I spent years fighting for, a protégé who I spent most of a career grooming will never run it, and at the precise moment I am to be publicly recognized for all of my decades of tireless effort and leadership, the vice president mixes me up with a restaurant chain. I suppose you'll chalk up my life as yet one more example of your hated government waste."

"It could have been different, Humphrey," Bader shrugged.

Humphrey laughed at the thought and shook his head. "No, it couldn't."

He had nearly arrived home when his cell phone rang. He recognized the number as a former staffer who had departed the agency a few years earlier to take a managerial position with the California Department of Food and Agriculture's Plant Health and Pest Prevention Services Division. They exchanged some pleasantries, and Humphrey's face brightened immensely.

"Why, yes, Jeff, I *am* available to provide management consultations," he beamed.

. . .

Jamie Caro-Marcus was happy to work in the new building. With the college tuition of her sons to think of, she knew she would be handling the same duties, planning the trips and conferences for all of the Agency of Invasive Species senior staff, until retirement. She found comfort in that assurance—most of the time.

One glaring exception was the night there was a documentary on the Reykjavik Summit, and she found herself thinking of all of the dreams—ambitious, silly, and otherwise—that ran through her head the first time she walked into the offices of the agency. She never had found the time to try to apply for a job with the United Nations, nor had any of the weed-related conferences she planned gotten her anywhere near the glamorous world of international diplomacy.

She called in sick the next day and decided she needed to see

Ava again. If she couldn't recapture how she felt then, she could at least cherish the same company as those days.

Jamie concluded it was a lot easier to get through each day if she didn't spend too much time thinking about what might have been.

DECEMBER 2012

Agency of Invasive Species Administrative Director Lisa Bloom differed from her two male predecessors. Despite all she had learned from Adam Humphrey and Jack Wilkins, she felt the agency and its dedicated employees needed to do a much better job of "telling their story." She found that the only way she could get press interested in telling that story was a free lunch.

So it was around a table at a Washington restaurant that she laid out the latest in weed abatement technology; the species the agency deemed most threatening to American agriculture; the public awareness campaigns they would unveil in the coming year. Most of the reporters faked interest, nodded, and ate, but there was one middle-aged guy at the end of the table with an increasingly amused and skeptical smirk.

Finally he piped up.

"As you know, as we speak, Congress and the president are grappling with the 'fiscal cliff' and sequester, and the forecast for the foreseeable future in Washington is an increasingly bitter fight among more and more hands over a stagnant funding pie," the reporter said. "The rating agencies are saying that another downgrade of the United States' credit rating could occur in the coming year if the federal government doesn't demonstrate an ability to control its long-term debt. Sooner or later, any government effort to control spending is going to look skeptically at a federal agency dedicated to fighting weeds. How concerned are you that fiscal realities might lead to dramatic cuts to your agency's budget or perhaps even eliminating your agency completely?"

Lisa greeted the question with laughter.

"I've been here a long time," she said. "I've heard that talk a lot of times before. We'll see if this time is any different."

ACKNOWLEDGMENTS

Dana Perino and Sean Desmond, both formerly of Crown Forum, got the ball rolling on this book, and I can't thank them enough. The ball was handed to Stephanie Knapp, without a fumble or wobble, in a manner so smooth and streamlined I'm still in disbelief. Campbell Wharton and the rest of the crew at Crown Forum are fantastic, and I am indebted to their efforts.

Whenever I mention that my agent is Mel Berger, eyebrows get raised, and I get the occasional, "Wait, why would he represent somebody like *you*?" I don't know why, but I'm very lucky to have him. On all the little details, I rest assured knowing Mel and his team have got things covered.

Way back in late 2011, Thomas Schatz and Leslie Page of Citizens Against Government Waste were kind enough to share their time and confirm all of my worst suspicions and fears about how the federal bureaucracy works and doesn't work. David Edwards, former executive director of the Joint National Committee for Languages, is an old Washington hand who knows where all the bodies were buried, and helped flesh out the portrait of the nation's capital in past decades.

I am very lucky to write for *National Review*, and bosses who will let you spread your wings, take risks, stumble, develop your voice, and pay you to do what you love, writing about politics. Thank you, Rich Lowry and Jack Fowler. My colleagues at *NR* are wonderful, brilliant, inspired people who are kind and warm enough to dispel my simmering jealousy of their talents.

Various friends read early drafts and saved me from my

worst instincts. Cam Edwards, Rachel Hanig Grunspan, Shannon Lane, Flint Dille, Amanda Seewald, thank you. Readers, if you encounter anything in these pages that stinks, it's because I ignored their advice in that spot.

As you read through this, you'll encounter happy-hour hangouts from 1990s-era Washington, and many, sadly, shut their doors years ago, but the memories of "the clique" and life as a low-level drone in the nation's capital will live forever. Okay, to be honest, some of those memories are a little fuzzy.

That illustration of Stalin with weeds in chapter one? That's the illustrative work of my brother Paul Geraghty, immensely talented. If you are holding this book right now, there is about a fifty percent chance my dad twisted your arm into buying it. He and my mom are gifts I don't deserve; the greatest unfair advantage any man ever had is parents who love him and provide role models.

Speaking of parenthood, my boys have been very patient. My older son, now six, can actually accurately describe the plot. Stay tuned for *The Weed Agency: The Animated Series!*

Finally, my wife, Allison, is the best, and she said she likes this book more than anything else I've ever written.*

---

* That isn't that high a bar to clear.

ABOUT THE AUTHOR

Jim Geraghty has been a contributing editor at *National Review* since 2004.

Previously a reporter at States News Service, Jim has written for the *Washington Post, Boston Globe, Denver Post, Detroit Free Press, Bergen Record,* and scores of other papers. Earlier in his career, he reported for the *Dallas Morning News,* Congressional Quarterly, and the now-departed websites Policy.com and Intellectual Capital.com.

His *Kerry Spot* blog was awarded "Best Political Dirt" by WashingtonPost.com in 2004, and the *Times* of London praised his "killer insight" in that election cycle.

Jim's first book, *Voting to Kill,* a look at how the 9/11 attacks affected American voters, was published by Simon and Schuster in August 2006. *Booklist* called the book "insightful and comprehensive," and David Reinhard's review in the *Oregonian* declared, "The reporting is fresh, the analysis rigorous and the writing snappy."

Jim spent two years in Ankara, Turkey, working as a foreign correspondent and studying anti-Americanism, democratization, Islam, Middle East politics, and U.S. diplomacy efforts, appearing in the *Philadelphia Inquirer, New York Sun, Washington Times,* and *Washington Examiner.* He covered violent protests over the Muhammad cartoons, avian flu outbreaks, and Pope Benedict XVI's visit to Ankara. He also covered national elections in Great Britain and Germany, and has reported from Egypt, Italy, Israel, Spain, and Jordan in his career.

In 2008, *Best Life* magazine called Jim one of "the 10 most important voices to listen to in this election cycle."

In addition to reporting and blogging, Jim regularly appears on *On the Record with Greta Van Susteren* and *Media Buzz with Howard Kurtz* on Fox News, Chuck Todd's *The Daily Rundown* on MSNBC, and *The Lead* with Jake Tapper on CNN.

Printed in the United States
by Baker & Taylor Publisher Services